This
Jesus of Nazareth
Without Money and Arms
Conquered More Millions Than
Alexander, Caesar, Mohammed, and Napoleon;
Without Science and Learning,
He Shed More Light on Things Human and Divine
Than All Philosophers and Scholars Combined;
Without the Eloquence of Schools,
He Spoke such Words of Life as
Were Never Spoken Before or Since,
And Produced Effects Which Lie Beyond
The Reach of Orator or Poet;
Without Writing a Single Line,
He Set More Pens in Motion,
And Furnished Themes for More Sermons,
Orations, Discussions, Learned Volumes,
Works of Art, and Songs of Praise
Than the Whole Army of Great Men
Of Ancient and Modern Times.

Philip Schaff, *"The Person of Christ"*
American Tract Society, 1913.

What Jesus Is Doing Through
Prayer Cookbook for Busy People Series

And John, calling two of his disciples to him, sent them to Jesus, saying, "Are you the coming One, or do we look for another?"

And that very hour He cured many of infirmities, afflictions, and evil spirits; and to many blind He gave sight.

Jesus answered and said to them, "Go and tell John the things you have seen and heard: that the blind see, the lame walk, the lepers are cleansed, the deaf hear, the dead are raised, the poor have the gospel preached to them. And blessed is he who is not offended because of Me."

Luke 7:19-23

"Endurance was one year eight months last month and was still sitting in one place unable to crawl around or walk, like many others at his age. From birth Endurance had the habit of always crying as from 11:45 PM to about 3 AM. For the rest of the night no sleep. The parents brought him to the clinic that I could pray for them and their baby. Thanks be to God I had a copy of the Prayer Cookbook. I took 3 days to journey with them through the book then we went into a 7-day prayer with fasting. In the second night of prayer, he stopped crying and could sleep almost all night. At the end of the prayer week, he crept for two days and five days after Endurance is running around. The parents have become Christians because of what they saw God do to them through Endurance."

**On behalf of the family,
Chaplain NJOBARA Hyacinth,
Bamenda, Cameroon**

"My husband has changed from a grumpy, complaining, discontented man for the past 31 years. Last year as I started using the prayer bullets in the Prayer Cookbook I have found a change in him. Elisha, it could not have been anything else but from the Prayer Cookbook. In actual fact, my husband is using the Prayer Cookbook too."

Seni L., Fiji Islands

"At that time I was being introduced to you, my younger sister was very sick, in a coma and everyone knew she was only going to die. I used your prayer points and she recovered. Due to this sickness she had lost her marriage, her job, her memory, her identity and almost all. Now she is well. She has two very good jobs (teacher and an editor with a Christian firm)."

Mariam A., United Arab Emirates

"I have never enjoyed my salvation like now. God is in Charge of my life and the Holy Spirit is leading me by the hand.

My husband was away in East Timor working on a UN mission for two months when I got access to your prayer manuals. Do you know he came back a changed husband and there is love all over. He wants to spend more and more time with me and consults me on everything—the opposite of what was before.

He even told me to identify a car for myself to buy. I thought he was not serious. Then he repeated it. I was trusting God for a car but I didn't know it would come like that—kingdom surprise!

While praying step four prayers in Prayer Cookbook for Busy People, *there is this prayer point where you say, "I shall be an arrow in the hand of God to bring healing to His people." God literally answered this one instantly. People have been waking me up very early in the morning to tell me their problems; many of them are marital problems and I would quickly introduce them to Golden Key prayers.*

I applied Golden key prayers to my neighbors' situation: a wife thrown out by her husband. Last Sunday, the 19th of August, she turned up at my house at six AM, she also confessed she does not know why she chose to come to me. I introduced her to the e-book, Point By Point, and she said she would do anything to get her marriage back.

She started the Esther fast on Tuesday, and by Saturday the husband was looking for her everywhere. All through I prayed for her as well and asked Jehovah to intervene and voila! On Monday this week, she came to my office with a testimony.

The same husband wants her back, no conditions. He has given her money and asked her to get a house to move in together!

Elisha, it works! God is still in the business of blessing people."

Lilian A., Kenya

"A friend of mine was given your web address by a workmate who was testifying of a breakthrough after doing the Esther Method for a brother who was dying but now has recovered.

When I got the address I was so happy because there are a lot of things I have been praying for but had not gotten the answers yet. I have grabbed the copy of Prayer Cookbook for Busy People *and have started some of the prayers . . ."*

Irene C., United Kingdom

"Sometime in December I stumbled on your website and I started receiving mail from you. I started using all the prayer points you send me and on New Year's Eve my children and I prayed using the 27 minutes to midnight prayer points. We continued our prayers in the new year and each time we prayed, we included the 40 prayer points to attract anything.

I had been separated from my husband of 17 years since February 2006, and our divorce was in the final stages but on the 21st of January 2008 we got back together. *My husband has received Jesus, and although he used to be against tithing, he is now tithing to a church in Africa which is desperately in need for funds to roof their church building. It is a miracle to see him do things like that. I give God the glory."*

Molly M., United Kingdom

"Last week my friends husband left her and told her not to contact him. I called her and she was in tears. I told her not to worry he would be back and I went on the Esther Fast and the prayer points from the Prayer Cookbook for Busy People. *On the sixth day, she sent me a message telling me that her husband was back home. Praise God and thanks for the books and prayer points."*

Norma P., United Kingdom

"Praise the Lord! During the weekend, a friend of mind almost committed suicide and I was sharing to her about the prayer points you mailed to me. I gave it to her and she was delivered from that spirit to commit suicide. Thank you so much. May God Bless Your Ministry."

Maraia M., Fiji Islands

"I fasted and prayed for the Lord to relieve me of my financial debts. These debts were like a noose around my neck and I was living from paycheck to paycheck. It is not yet ninety days and God has answered my prayer. My mountain of debt was ninety-thousand dollars (90,000), and 'Glory to God' all my debts are paid and not only that, I now have thirty-thousand (30,000) dollars in the bank."

Sandra D., Belize

"The materials you have sent me are just great. I had read so many books on prayer before but none of them led me to pray. In the last few days I have been drawn so close to the Lord. Thanks for the revealed keys.

I first learned of you when I visited my sister in hospital mid this month. She was due for surgery and her friends from church visited her and gave her your Prayer Cookbook *and asked her to pray at midnight. She had a successful surgery and her recovery is so quick. She is not just healed physically, she is revived spirit, soul and body.*

I now want to know all that you have to share with me. I never really liked praying but I suddenly have a passion to do so."

Margaret W., Kenya

"I would just like to thank you for the e-book, Prayer Cookbook for Busy People. *Since I have started putting the prayer points into practice, God has blessed my husband with a job relocation and also they increased his hourly salary rate. I thank GOD immensely for answering my prayers. GOD is AWESOME, WONDERFUL AND FAITHFUL.*

GOD has also blessed me in the area of my Health, for the past year I have suffered with intense abdominal cramps every month, so intense that I could not function at work, walk, sit or even lie down when I started the prayer and fast and praying over my organs, intestines and whole body, I realized that is month I was free of pain and working as any other day. I could not stop thanking GOD for HIS BLESSINGS and HIS MERCY.

GOD has blessed you with a great and magnificent gift. Thank you again for your prayer points."

Jenelle D., Trinidad

"A lot of things have changed in my life since I joined you in the prayer marathon last year. Not that I received thousands of euros (yet) but many little things in my spiritual life with the Lord—breakthroughs in my thinking, my understanding of leadership and authority and also more insight in how much the Lord loves me, His child. The best part is that I broke free from a condemnation spirit that kept me going and doubting for years. So thanks for all your hard work and educating the body of Christ."

Rosette S., Belgium

"You have really taught me to pray. I have been sending your prayer marathon to my sisters and friends and they are experiencing tremendous change in their lives too. I have not only been blessed financially, but my relationship with people is just getting better and better."

Joan G., Denmark

"In August 2005 my husband and I were struggling financially to close the deal on a home that we had purchased. We could not get anywhere. One day I came in contact with your email; I can't remember how but it was a blessing. Today, we are victorious. The deal has closed and the home is released to us. To God be the Glory."

Geraldine B., Jamaica

"This is Annie. Remember me? You had taught me to pray. During the Prayer Riot Phase 2, I kept confessing and praying the prayer points for my daughter who was asked to wear glasses at the age of 2 (her power for both eyes were minus 2.5). Because she was too small, she did not wear one. Now during this prayer time she was taken to an optician from her school and the report came totally clean that she has perfect eye sight and she does not have to wear glasses."

Annie A., Muscat

"I can't thank you enough for everything that you have taught me on prayer. My husband has been delivered from alcoholism and is now growing spiritually and God has taken me to another spiritual level."

Glenda M., California

"I am so elated!!! Remember my 'frustrated firstlady' letter I sent you? You told me to use my problems as an opportunity that God can use to teach 'your hands to war and your fingers to fight.' Well Elisha, the Prayer Marathon taught me just how to do that. The Lord opened up my understanding so much and gave me victory! I cannot believe that in such a short time since I started the marathon, within the second week I was having victories even with my marriage. Right now my husband is the sweetest thing . . . It's like we just got married!"

Empowered Lady, Canada

"I have been praying for a car. All the banks were declining to approve me for vehicle finance because I am not a South African citizen and I only have a temporary work permit. Now I started claiming my car in the Name of Jesus and started binding every hindering forces as you taught. I went on the three days fast. I only managed 2 days and 1 night but I have received my answer. The CEO from overseas actually phoned me to say that the Company is buying a car for me"

Memory M., South Africa

"I have heard so much about you. In September 2007, a close friend sent me your prayer points for single women. I did pray regularly and guess u what, the Lord did it; I got married on 7th June this year at a very lovely function and we give God all the glory.

As a newly married lady, I'd like to dedicate my marriage to God and start praying for it. Thanks and God bless you."

Irene K., Zimbabwe

"Hi Elisha I want to tell you that your prayer points are really working.

My friend told me about your site on the 27 of May 2008, when I was from the interview. During the interview I did very bad and the devil tried to discourage me that I was not going to get the job. Then I started using the prayer point and I bought the Prayer Cookbook for Busy People *then I used I even used the Esther method from the 6th of June till the 8th of June.*

Hey Elisha! On the 10th of June I received a call. They said I got the job. Is this not wonderful? Yes our God is wonderful."

Mandlenkosi S., South Africa

"God is doing amazing things. A month ago a lady called Mary walked up to me after church and asked me to pray with her because she had a job interview with UNDP on Tuesday of that week. She was a stranger to me. I asked her to fast and arranged to meet the next day in the evening to pray. We met the next evening and I handed her the prayer points in the Prayer Cookbook: 27 Prayers That Bring You Success In Competition. *I asked her to pray at midnight and I also set aside midnight to pray with her.*

Last week she called me and told me she had gotten the job and was called to sign the contract. It happened so fast. I give glory to God. Elisha, I thank God for you. Every piece of information I have read from you has transformed my life."

Esther B., Uganda

"Finally, I want to thank God that through your guidance the Lord has opened doors that I never imagined would ever be opened. The Lord blessed me with a new job on the 4th month of coming across your learning materials and by His grace, diligently seeking and applying. I had all my debts cleared and have had some change to invest.

In addition, I have had the bank approve a mortgage, something I had not even dreamt of. I continue to stand in awe at what the Lord can do when you learn how to engage Him. (PS, gave my life to Christ over 20 years and endeavored to live by the Book but never before had such a tremendous breakthrough in a very short space of time). Targeted prayers that yield anticipated results had never been so real in a big scale such as this. May God continue to use you to help many more out of the mire we have lived in for years on end."

Georgina S., United Kingdom

"I have so much to say I am not sure where to begin. I believe the Holy Spirit led me to you site last year so that I can learn how to fight. You might remember my desperate email last year. Where my fiancée did not want to go to church anymore and he refused to get married. Elisha, since that time I have had great victories and battles but I have won them all.

We are now married he goes to church without question and last night, bless the lord, he gave his tithes for the first time in his life, coming from a Catholic background he did not believe in tithing. It's as though God completely turned this man around almost a year ago. I remember you emailing me and telling me it won't be an easy battle. Thank God!"

Sister K.J., Grenada

"I will not forget to share this one with you. First I went on Esther fast with Psalm 2, as described in the book. That was in October 2006 and within days doors that had refused to open for over eight years of marriage, began to open. God is good, I weep with joy as I type this email. After my wedding in 1998 everything about my husband stood still, my dear, which will I say, people even termed me to be a bad luck to him, But to the glory of God, He did it for me, just within three months. My husband was able to buy a car and a piece of land where we are now setting up our building, and so many other things. It was so much, that was why I pressed on for your e-books. May God richly bless you, and increase you knowledge."

Florence D., Nigeria

"I have no words to thank our Lord and yourself for the most valuable prayer points/breakthroughs/information you emailed to me. The Lord has healed me from cancer too. The doctor said I am a miracle, but doctor I am serving a miracle God!!

My relationship with the Lord is now so close and He already answered my prayers. I can see the mighty change in my marriage. I also told my family/friends and their prayer results are just so amazing."

Lorraine V., South Africa

"I write to testify of the goodness of God in restoring my marriage. I engaged in a 21-day Prayer Marathon using the prayer points for singles but substituted wherever it mentioned 'singles' for my own needs. **I was so much inspired by the Prayer Cookbook extract and the Dream Code**. *I read everything you sent during the Singles Prayer Marathon.*

These prayers resulted in a 'spiritual drama' manifestation. One of the days it happened like 'a madman whose sanity had just been restored,' and my husband suddenly came back to his senses. He confessed all that he had done (by the way I knew it all but had kept most of it to myself) and he literally knelt down begging me to forgive him and promised to make it up for the lost time. In a shock, I was stunned."

Memory G., Zimbabwe

"I have been depressed for a long time and the first night I prayed for deliverance from depression, I feel like a weight has been lifted from my shoulders. I feel like a new person."

Nkazana S., Zimbabwe

"Elisha, I would like to share with you the great transformation that happened just after two weeks of my participation in midnight prayers. I have never opened my mouth in my one and a half years of being a new team leader in all the managers meeting that I attended. But on Thursday 2/02 and again 10/02, in our managers meeting I raised a few points. Not only were they minor but they were the best as I received positive remarks from my peers and my manager was really shocked. Thank you Elisha, and I thank the almighty for being there for me. Thank you Lord Jesus."

Kesaia R., Australia

"Just to mention but a few, I have experienced a breakthrough in my health and my spiritual life has catapulted to the mountain top just in three months.

As a minister, it's amazing how much anointing has come upon me since I intensively engaged your prayers. The manifestation is so mighty and tangible every time I preach, and the recent example is just this Easter when I was preaching."

Anikie M., Botswana

"I prayed that prayer bullet aggressively and with tears as I desperately wanted breakthroughs in my prayers.

I didn't know where the breakthrough was going to come from but my heart's desire this year is that my husband and three children would surrender to Jesus, make Him Lord and Saviour of their lives and be used to extend His Kingdom and bring Glory to Him. That is truly my deep heart's desire.

On Resurrection Sunday, at the end of our church service, my 11-year old daughter responded of her own free will to the altar call made by the pastor."

Cathy L., Fiji

"I went to minister to a family who are drought hit. I read the Word of God and launched cover prayer points by the time we finished, the whole family accepted Christ."

Rev Francis, Kenya

"My relationship with my mother has been restored after 30 years since I started praying these prayers. The same thing with my son and only child. Both have been given back to me."

Sister Mary, Florida

"I love praying for others, The Lord just healed a lady that I prayed for using the bullets you teach me. They had given her three months of life because of brain cancer. Several of us prayed and she went to surgery today, the doctors were amazed, they took the tumor out and nothing left. Glory to Jesus."

Tatty W., Georgia

"I got to know about you on the 14th day of the singles prayer marathon after an excited friend told me about you and she had two of your books, Prayer DNA Secrets and Prayer Cookbook for Busy People. *I downloaded The 9 Mistakes booklet and distributed it to over 10 singles who I knew needed help. One lady I gave it to had tried about four times to marry but to no avail. They attempted to wed four times and every time the weddings would be cancelled. Since I caught the marathon midway, I only managed to get days 14 through 21 and days 2, 3, 4, 10, 11, and 12, which were weekends. Those prayer points were enough to get her the victory and the good news is they finally wedded on Friday the 27th of October, to the Glory of God."*

Name Withheld on Request

"I discovered your site while looking for self-deliverance prayer points on the web. My wedding, which was scheduled for the earlier part of this year, was mysteriously and embarrassingly cancelled by my fiancé a week before the event. When you started emailing me, I then understood that an evil gate had been opened against me at midnight. I have used your prayer points in addition to other instructions from the Lord and praise God, I got married first week in September!"

Vikki M., United Kingdom

RAINMAKER'S PREYER

Featuring the "Miracle Magnetizer" Prayer Sequence to help you break fresh grounds in every area of life . . . regardless of your present situation in 90 days or less.

ELISHA GOODMAN

Internet's #1 Prayer Coach
www.firesprings.com

Contents

OTHER BOOKS IN THE SERIES

*"Rainmaker's Prayer is like food.
It is essential and sustaining."*

Elisha Goodman

NEW YEAR'S SHOCKER . . .
"PHYSICIAN, HEAL THYSELF!"

"It's over . . . finished!" she sobbed.
"The doctors have already tried everything.
None of the pastors we know seem to be
available now, in our moment of need.
I don't know what to do anymore!"

$\mathcal{I}$t was only the first day of the New Year and I was in shock. Receiving news of a death in the family was no way to start the year. I was stunned, especially since we were still on a three-day Esther Fast, praying about this situation, among many other things.

But now the voice on the other end of the line was saying, "Look, in spite of your prayer and fasting, your father-in-law is dead and gone."

He had been sick for months. The doctors couldn't quite decide whether it was diabetes or something else entirely. I hadn't seen him in a few years—even now we were separated by thousands of miles.

In my absence I had arranged for ministers of God to visit his bedside regularly. From the reports, things didn't look too good. At age 79, his health was deteriorating fast. For many years, he was a prayer warrior himself, but now he was at a point where he could not muster the strength to pray.

He was getting worse, not better.

All the same, it came as a rude shock to hear he was gone.

Or was he?

A few minutes passed and I was still feeling numb from the news I had just received. It was then when I heard the clear, unmistakable voice of the Holy Spirit, with this strange marching order:

"Get up! Take your wedding photograph . . . the one at the church with your father-in-law . . . anoint it and pray as I'm going to direct you now!"

I thought to myself, "That old wedding picture?"

This was intriguing. My mind was in a fog. I remembered seeing it a few weeks earlier, somewhere. It wasn't even framed—just one of many old photos scattered around the house.

For about ten minutes, we frantically searched throughout the house, but it was nowhere to be found. Anxious to get started with the prayers, I led the way downstairs to the family prayer altar. There, we began to pray. And pray. And pray.

Nothing happened. No one received any special revelation.

In the back of my mind, I knew something was missing. Deep down in my spirit I kept hearing the words: wedding picture . . . wedding picture . . . wedding picture.

After an hour of prayer, it was clear to me that we were not making much progress. So I called a break. I wanted to go search for the picture that the Lord told us we needed to use as a point of contact.

It was now one o'clock in the afternoon. I decided we would resume praying at four o'clock. That should be enough time to find the picture, I reasoned.

Again, we searched exhaustively but found nothing.

At 4:00 PM, we were forced to return to prayer without the photograph. Ten minutes into the praise and worship session, I heard someone shout a loud, "Praise the Lord, thank you Jesus!"

In an instant, my spouse was off, running up the stairs. A moment later, she returned with the picture in hand.

She later told us that as we were worshiping the Lord her eyes were "opened in the spirit" and she saw where the picture had been all along!

Then the action began.

As soon as I anointed the picture and laid my hands on the image of my father-in-law, my eyes too opened in the spirit.

The prayers came fast and furious. As the first prayer point was dropped in my spirit, we began to pray. Then I received the second one, then the third one.

Suddenly, a strong wind began to blow in the spirit. As I watched, what appeared to be a grave was pushed open with a great force. Out jumped a young looking man, perhaps in his late thirties. He began to sprint away, arms raised up in the air, rejoicing. When I looked closely at the man, I thought this could have been a much younger version of my father-in-law.

At that moment I knew that the man would live and not die. Immediately we changed the realm of the prayers, and then went into an extended session of praise and worship, thanking the Lord for His faithfulness. We had one more session of prayers at 9:00 PM. Then we went to bed.

At exactly midnight, the phone rang. Seconds later I was hearing shouts of "Hallelujah! Praise the Lord!"

I jumped up from bed, ran out and grabbed the phone from my daughter's outstretched hand. That's when I heard the reassuring voice of my father-in-law saying, "We serve the Living God; praise His name forever!"

His voice sounded stronger than I had heard it in years. He went on to tell us how the Lord delivered him from the powers of the grave. I was speechless.

As I write this, my father-in-law is still alive and on his way to full recovery.

Praise Jesus Christ.

The Lord laid it on my heart to share the story in this manual. He did so for a purpose. He particularly wanted me to include the three *resurrection* prayer arrows that were released to me during the heat of battle. You will find them "embedded" in the Prayershock section starting from page 134.

I should point out that each prayer for the 21-day coaching session was divinely released—though admittedly not in such dramatic circumstances as the one I've just recounted.

The Lord made me to understand that the situation of my father-in-law on January 1st is the exact same situation that most believers are in today: they are in a state of satanic burial.

For some it is their health. In fact, many physical afflictions that some people are struggling with have their roots deep in in the spiritual.

For others it is their marriage. Trafficking spirits have somehow stolen the honey of their marriage, leaving behind a trail of problems, strife, and distress.

For a vast majority of people, their finances are suffering. While they are trying to figure out what went wrong, every day some invisible powers are busy swallowing their divine benefits in the spirit. Many have yet to realize that the enemy has just launched a massive economic war against the inhabitants of the earth.

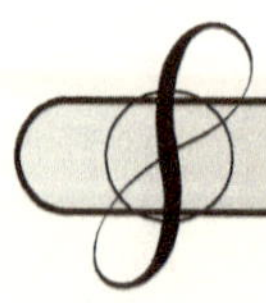

Why? Because this enemy wants to control all the wealth and resources that the Lord has freely provided for his people.

I am all fired up in my spirit right now. The hammer of the Holy Ghost is about to strike down hard upon the head of the wicked. For far too long, many of God's children have had to wander the spiritual wilderness with a tin cup and a tambourine, dancing for mere crumbs of bread just to survive from day to day. Meanwhile the devil and his agents, relying on a toxic mixture of ignorance and sin, have been busy drinking their blood and sharing out their God-given virtues in the spirit without their knowledge.

The Lord is about to turn the tables against these powers.

In the prayer session that follows, you will discover how to pray what we call *Miracle Magnetizer* prayers.

- The kinds of prayers that brought my father-in-law back from the dead on January 1st.
- The kinds of prayers that bring rain, even in the midst of a devastating famine.
- The kinds of prayers that will provoke heaven's direct intervention and help you break fresh grounds in the days ahead.

But first, let me lay the groundwork by looking at the two kinds of prayer that Jesus taught.

Unknown to most people, the Lord Jesus taught two kinds of prayers back to back. The first is universally known as the "Lord's Prayer." I'm not going to teach you the Lord's Prayer. You can (and should) learn this elsewhere.

The second type is something else entirely. Not understanding the difference between the two (and when to use them) has crushed the faith of many and cut them off from operating in the realm of true anointing and power.

From this point, we're going to be moving at a fast pace. You'll find the very next section, *Jesus Teaches Two Kinds of Prayer*, a useful foundation for all the subsequent material, especially if you've never known the difference between the prayers of war and peace.

Chapter One

Jesus Teaches Two Kinds of Prayer

I'd like us to begin with a prayer. Please bow down your head, close your eyes if you can, and take this prayer with fire in your spirit:

> *"O LORD, open my eyes and ears, and grant me spiritual understanding in the name of Jesus."*

When I was young, my mother taught me to pray. First she taught me to share the grace before meals. I became so good at this that my siblings used to joke that any day I forgot to pray on my food, they would have to call the doctor to see if I was okay.

In church, they taught us the Lord's Prayer. Even in school, the teachers made sure we all knew how to pray. In Sunday school, we recited the Lord's Prayer so many times it became second nature to us. As a result, I went around for decades believing I knew how to pray.

And I continued to believe I knew until one day disaster struck. I realized then that I needed help. I came to the painful realization that there was something seriously wrong with the way I'd been praying all along. But before I tell you all about that, let's go to the scripture.

In Luke, chapter eleven, we see Jesus teaching his disciples to pray.

So He said to them,
"When you pray, say:
Our Father in heaven,
Hallowed be Your name.
Your kingdom come.
Your will be done
On earth as it is in heaven.

Give us day by day our daily bread.
And forgive us our sins,
For we also forgive everyone who is indebted to us.
And do not lead us into temptation,

But deliver us from the evil one."

And He said to them,

"Which of you shall have a friend,
and go to him at midnight and say to him,
'Friend, lend me three loaves;

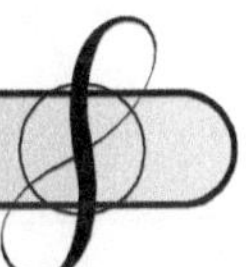

> *for a friend of mine has come to me on his journey,*
> *and I have nothing to set before him';*
>
> *and he will answer from within and say,*
> *'Do not trouble me; the door is now shut,*
> *and my children are with me in bed;*
> *I cannot rise and give to you'?*
>
> *I say to you, though he will not rise*
> *and give to him because he is his friend,*
> *yet because of his persistence he will rise*
> *and give him as many as he needs."*
>
> *"So I say to you, ask, and it will be given to you;*
> *seek, and you will find; knock, and it will be opened to you."*
>
> *For everyone who asks receives, and he who seeks finds,*
> *and to him who knocks it will be opened.*
>
> *Luke 11:2-11*

In verses two to four, we see a framework; a model of one type of prayer. In fact, this model is so popular most people believe that's the only way Jesus ever taught us to pray. Hundreds, if not thousands of books and sermons exist to support and clarify this model of prayer.

For instance, a best-selling book on prayer (a million copies in print) cleverly breaks things down using a simple acronym, A-C-T-S, in which the letters stand for:

A – Adoration
C – Confession
T – Thanksgiving
S – Supplication

Using this model, start your prayer with adoration, praise and worship unto the Lord. This is followed by confession of sins and asking Him for forgiveness. (The sins are to be confessed one by one, not in some vague or generalized manner.) Next comes thanksgiving for what the Lord has already done. Finally, you bring your requests before the Lord, asking for His help, not just for yourself, but for others in need.

4 Alphabet of Praise

Recently a woman of God was taking a Sunday school class through ACTS. She focused on the Adoration segment and came up with what she called an alphabet of praise. She asked each one of us to think of attributes of God, each beginning with a different letter of the alphabet. We then had to use those attributes (in alphabetical order) to praise the Lord specifically in prayer.

Our class came up with the following words of adoration:

A – **Almighty**	**D** – **Divine**
B – **Blessed Redeemer**	**E** – **Everlasting**
C – **Caring**	**F** – **Faithful**

G –	**G**lorious	**Q** –	**Q**uick
H –	**H**oly	**R** –	**R**ighteous
I –	**I**nfinite	**S** –	**S**avior
J –	**J**ust	**T** –	**T**rustworthy
K –	**K**ing	**U** –	**U**nity (Father, Son, Holy Ghost)
L –	**L**oving	**V** –	**V**ictorious
M –	**M**ighty	**W** –	**W**onderful
N –	**N**oble	**X** –	E**x**alted
O –	**O**mnipotent	**Y** –	**Y**earning (for sinners to repent)
P –	**P**owerful	**Z** –	**Z**ealous

We then proceeded to praise the Lord, using these words. I can attest that we all had a wonderful experience.

Now this is the first kind of prayer that Jesus taught. I call it a *Type 1 prayer*. This is the kind of prayer you use when all is going well.

Type 1 Prayers—When Things Are Going Pretty Well

It is very easy to forget that *not* everyone is going through difficult times and seasons in their lives. While some are going through severe storms in their lives—finances, health, relationships—others are seeing times of plenty and prosperity, even today.

The scripture confirms this in the book of Ecclesiastes, Chapter 3:

To everything there is a season,
A time for every purpose under heaven:
A time to be born,
And a time to die;
A time to plant,
And a time to pluck what is planted;
A time to kill,
And a time to heal;
A time to break down,
And a time to build up;
A time to weep,
And a time to laugh;
A time to mourn,
And a time to dance;
A time to cast away stones,
And a time to gather stones;
A time to embrace,
And a time to refrain from embracing;
A time to gain,
And a time to lose;
A time to keep,

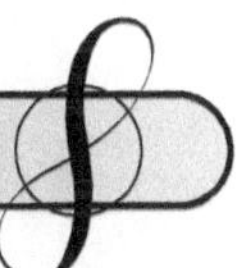

> *And a time to throw away;*
> *A time to tear,*
> *And a time to sew;*
> *A time to keep silence,*
> *And a time to speak;*
> *A time to love,*
> *And a time to hate;*
> *A time of war,*
> *And a time of peace.*
>
> *Eccl 3:1-8*

When everything appears to be going well, it is important to maintain unbroken communication with the Lord, day in and day out.

This Type 1 prayer helps us keep our communication lines with the Lord open. It moves us closer to Him every day. And as we commune with Him and immerse ourselves in His word, a transformation begins to take place. We find ourselves going deeper and deeper in our level of intimacy with Him. And He begins to take us into confidence and share divine secrets with us.

Praise the Lord.

Yet, as important as this prayer model is to a believer, it still does not go far enough. It only tells half the story. Our Lord Jesus did not want to leave us with the impression that that was all there is to prayer. So He quickly followed up with what I call *Type 2 prayer.*

As a matter of fact, Jesus considered this next model of prayer so crucial that He resorted to using a parable, as He so often did when He wanted to reveal a profound truth in a way that only those with spiritual ears could understand.

Here is the parable from verse 5:

And He said to them,
"Which of you shall have a friend,
and go to him at midnight and say to him,

'Friend, lend me three loaves;
for a friend of mine has come to me on his journey,
and I have nothing to set before him';

and he will answer from within and say,
'Do not trouble me; the door is now shut,
and my children are with me in bed;
I cannot rise and give to you'?

I say to you, though he will not rise
and give to him because he is his friend,
yet because of his persistence he will rise
and give him as many as he needs.

So I say to you, ask, and it will be given to you;
seek, and you will find; knock, and it will be opened to you.
For everyone who asks receives, and he who seeks finds,
and to him who knocks it will be opened."

Luke 11:5-10

8

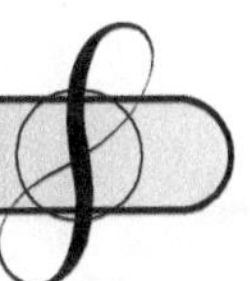

Please watch this carefully. Our Lord recognized that there are situations we face in life that would require a different approach to prayer.

An aggressive approach.
A desperate approach.
A persistent, unrelenting, never-give-up approach.

This is why He did not stop with the Lord's Prayer. He went further, as we are about to see shortly.

Type 2 Prayers—When All Is Not Going Well

A wise man has said, "the ultimate measure of a person is not where he stands in the moment of comfort and convenience, but where he stands at times of challenge and controversy."

Recall that in the parable of Jesus, the central character suddenly finds himself in a challenging situation in the middle of the night. In desperation he rushes to his friend to ask for help. The friend has every right (and many good reasons) to refuse the request. But the Lord is teaching us here that none of that mattered. This bold, desperate man had to get what he wanted.

At times many believers find it difficult to wrap their arms around this one parable. We may never know whether this desperate man was a good person or a very bad fellow. Nothing is said about his spiritual background or his family heritage. All that is relevant to the narrative is that he took bold and desperately urgent action when suddenly confronted with a crisis.

To put it another way:

- He took immediate and decisive action.
- He knew exactly where to seek help.
- He wasn't prepared to take "No" for an answer.

Out of this parable flows this eternal truth:

> *"So I say to you, ask, and it will be given to you;*
> *seek, and you will find; knock, and it will be opened to you."*

For everyone who asks, receives; and he who seeks, finds; and to him who knocks, it will be opened.

Beloved, if you are reading this, Jesus wants you to know that when you are confronted with the storms of life, you have His permission to do what this man did—take bold desperate action in prayer. He wants you to know that at such times, you need to progress beyond the A-C-T-S level of prayer.

You will be able to apply the principles of this parable, with boldness, persistence and aggression until the answer comes—once you take care of one little mistake . . .

Free 21-day prayer coaching program details are available on our website: *www.1christianbook.com/blog* by using the following details:

Email: guest@firesprings.com **Password:** 17a18K73b95M

Chapter Two

One Deadly Mistake You Must Never Make

If what you've read so far sounds contrary to all you have been taught in the past about prayer, please stay with me for a few minutes. You are about to see from scripture why prayers of adoration, praise, and worship may not be enough to address some of the urgent issues that are confronting so many people today.

Jumping right back into scripture, we begin our reading from the book of Job:

> *And the LORD said unto Satan, "Behold, all that he hath is in thy power; only upon himself put not forth thine hand." So Satan went forth from the presence of the LORD.*

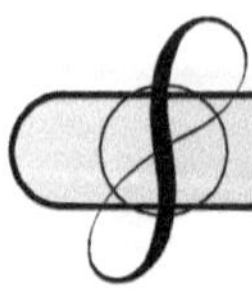

And there was a day when his sons and his daughters were eating and drinking wine in their eldest brother's house:

And there came a messenger unto Job, and said, "The oxen were plowing, and the asses feeding beside them:

And the Sabeans fell upon them, and took them away; yea, they have slain the servants with the edge of the sword; and I only am escaped alone to tell thee."

While he was yet speaking, there came also another, and said, "The fire of God is fallen from heaven, and hath burned up the sheep, and the servants, and consumed them; and I only am escaped alone to tell thee."

While he was yet speaking, there came also another, and said, "The Chaldeans made out three bands, and fell upon the camels, and have carried them away, yea, and slain the servants with the edge of the sword; and I only am escaped alone to tell thee."

While he was yet speaking, there came also another, and said, "Thy sons and thy daughters were eating and drinking wine in their eldest brother's house:

And, behold, there came a great wind from the wilderness, and smote the four corners of the house, and it fell upon the young men, and they are dead; and I only am escaped alone to tell thee."

> *Then Job arose, and rent his mantle, and shaved his head, and fell down upon the ground, and worshipped,*
>
> *And said, "Naked came I out of my mother's womb, and naked shall I return thither: the LORD gave, and the LORD hath taken away; blessed be the name of the LORD."*
>
> *Job 1:12-21*

Please read the last two verses again—very slowly.

This righteous man, Job, in spite of all the afflictions with which the enemy was bombarding him, was still able to bow his head and worship the Lord. No wonder the Lord was so confident in him!

But as you continue to study the book of Job, and as this drama played out yet further, two things become disturbingly clear:

1. The problems did not go away.
2. Job's problems actually intensified and took on a more frightening dimension.

This becomes more of an academic exercise. You begin to wonder what would have happened if indeed Job had advanced into another realm of prayer, just as Jesus taught. Would the problems have been prolonged to the extent that we read about?

We will never know the answer to this. But one thing is certain and it is this: by the time the Lord wanted to roll away his reproach, He gave a mysterious instruction that was related to prayer. Let's read it together:

> *"Therefore take unto you now seven bullocks and seven rams, and go to my servant Job, and offer up for yourselves a burnt offering; and my servant Job shall pray for you: for him will I accept: lest I deal with you after your folly, in that ye have not spoken of me the thing which is right, like my servant Job."*
>
> *So Eliphaz the Temanite and Bildad the Shuhite and Zophar the Naamathite went, and did according as the LORD commanded them: the LORD also accepted Job.*
>
> *And the LORD turned the captivity of Job, when he prayed for his friends: also the LORD gave Job twice as much as he had before.*
>
> *Job 42:8-10*

Did you see it? Terrible afflictions may never end without prayer birthed in the heart of God. For the Lord to move in this situation, Job had to fall back on the old trusted weapon of prayer. In fact, he had to change the way he had been praying. He had to change the focus of his prayer. He had to enter into another realm of prayer because up until now, the rantings of his friends did not help. The complaining and murmuring did not help. Nothing else worked.

14

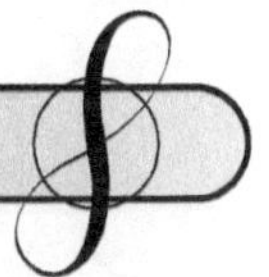

Only a specific kind of prayer, originating from the heart of God, was required to put an end to the problem.

Only prayer: another realm of prayer.

The scripture abounds with powerful examples of people who entered into another realm of prayer at the moment of great crisis. Upon entering that realm, the Lord turned their captivity around.

The "Prayer Hall of Fame" is jam-packed with bold, desperate men and women who at some point or the other needed urgent, divine intervention at a time of personal or national crisis, such as:

- Hannah praying for a child
- Moses confronting the Red Sea
- Elijah confronting 400 prophets of Baal
- The desperate cry of Blind Bartimaeus to Jesus
- The apostles in Acts, chapter 4
- The Lord Jesus at the garden of Gethsemane

That was the realm of prayer into which the Lord moved us on that fateful first day of January as we interceded for my father-in-law, who lay dying thousands of miles away, as I described in the opening pages of this book. My prayer for you reading this is that the Eternal Rock of Ages will promote you into this exciting new realm of prayer in Jesus' mighty name.

Back to Job.

It should be noted that when Job prayed as he was directed by the Lord, his long-term problems disappeared and restoration came.

But here's one deadly mistake that is common these days:

When a situation has deep roots in the spiritual realm (such as that of Job) some people do not immediately see the need to change their realm of prayer in order to address it squarely.

All the flowing, uplifting, and religious-sounding Type 1 prayers we discussed earlier may not be appropriate, particularly if one is facing a satanic "shock-and-awe" operation orchestrated from the realm of the spirit.

One thing should be clear by now. Every Christian, at one time or another, will be forced to confront what the Bible calls, "the time of Jacob's trouble."

Based upon the thousands of emails I receive, many people are in the thick of it right now, as you read this. Others have successfully overcome tough situations in the past, with the help of the Holy Spirit. But there's no telling what will arise in the days ahead.

If you diligently study and apply the three key principles presented in the next few chapters, you will have a front row seat as we prepare to carry out the last-minute instruction of Jesus detailed in Chapter 8.

But first, a conversation from hell . . .

Chapter Three

A Conversation From Hell

*a*s I mentioned at the close of Chapter 2, I receive a lot
of emails. Even as I write this I am looking at just one of
several email boxes.

Here's the vital statistics:

○ Total number of emails received: 74,028
○ Number of unopened emails: 14,376
○ Total number of praise reports: 2,003

And this is just one out of many addresses; the very first
address I established long ago, back in 2005 when the site,
www.firesprings.com, went live.

Many of the issues addressed in the *Prayer Cookbook*^{TM}
Series and newsletters are drawn from real life, everyday
issues with which many believers are struggling today. To
give you a vivid example, let me present a conversation that
took place on January 20th at 3:35 PM. It appeared in my
inbox a few moments later. The conversation is between an
unmarried Christian sister and her strange boyfriend.

(Actual names have been changed in order to protect the identity of individuals.)

Please read through it and see if you can identify the danger signals. Try not to look at my comments at the end of the conversation before you've made an attempt on your own.

Date: Tuesday, January 20th

Christian Sister:	It's always good to be honest to oneself. If things are not working out, there is no need to stress yourself
Boyfriend:	i don't jump from gal to gal seeking happiness
Christian Sister:	Neither did i say so, i prefer ending relationships on a good note
Boyfriend:	go on i mean you are used to that, am not the first one u are dumping am sure
Christian Sister:	I don't want a life where am always being shouted at, being blamed for unnecessary stuff
Boyfriend:	save me that

Christian Sister:	You are not happy with me, so i don't see the point of making miserable anymore am glad it you mention this i thought so anyway. i could tell from the kind of attitude u were pulling out
Boyfriend:	if that's how u are used to treating men am not that type. u got a wrong man to practise that on
Christian Sister:	what are u going to do, kill me?
Boyfriend:	things are very complicated ryt now
Christian Sister:	the way u have handled this whole thing, just makes me wonder u know i want to settle down one day with a guy, who will love me and appreciate me, not always arguing. i would even rather be alone than be with someone but miserable
Boyfriend:	ok ok ok. quit do whatever u want fine
Christian Sister:	of late it has really been impossible for us to have a normal conversation
Boyfriend:	let me not drag you into things u can hardly understand

Christian Sister: and what don't i understand?

Boyfriend: who u are involved with

Christian Sister: yes some mystery being?

Boyfriend: every thing works with time

Christian Sister: no one will be prepared to marry something they do not know

Boyfriend: fine i can live this way. i have always lived like this and am still here

Christian Sister: from your home, your relatives, your friends, yourself . . . everything is secret

Boyfriend: ok that's interesting

Christian Sister: u are embarrassed of me

Boyfriend: u are now telling me that, are u trying to be a jerk or what?

Christian Sister: Anyway I think i will end here, some of us are not used to such kinds of language

Boyfriend: sorry, well u just have no idea of what am going thru ryt now, the last thing i want to do is get it all out on u ryt now, but since u are out i will handle it all alone

Christian Sister: You are not ready for a relationship, that's all i can say u are not accommodating. u do whatever please u, u always do whatever pleases u with no regard of how your friend could be feeling

Boyfriend: u are forgetting one thing, if i meant evil to you did i use u?

Christian Sister: even in mere friendship always put yourself in the other person's shoes love is a feeling that makes u want to do more for the other person

Boyfriend: if you think u were going to resist u are wrong, i was going to do whatever i wanted if only i didn't respect u

Christian Sister: what is that supposed to mean?

Boyfriend   u are saying i was not considerate

Christian Sister: i didn't say u meant evil, it's your attitude which is a problem

Boyfriend: attitude problem me?

Christian Sister: being considerate does not mean only in the area of sex, but in everything. The way u respond me, what u do etc. how u handle issues as they come along

Boyfriend:	but it's the end, young woman. u have just drawn the battle line
Christian Sister:	yeah and bye
Boyfriend:	u just managed to break my heart, i won't break yours i will do worse
Christian Sister:	We come from 2 different worlds
Boyfriend:	break
Christian Sister:	meaning?
Boyfriend:	u have created war and so it shall be
Christian Sister:	a heart can only break when that person meant something to u, not otherwise. And who are u going to fight with? i believe in leaving people in one piece, u believe in destroying
Boyfriend:	fools rush in where angels fear to tread. u lit the fire burning in my heart
Christian Sister:	but be assured u won't destroy me, because my Jesus did not end on the cross, i have His protection, since u have declared war, it's not me u are going to face. It's the Lord Himself

22

Boyfriend:	lets wait and see
Christian Sister:	You are wolf in a sheep's skin. read 2 Timothy 4:18
Boyfriend:	i hope you think as much as you talk. for u shall be punished at the sea of holy fire for your devilish ways
Christian Sister:	No wonder u couldn't reveal your residence, your home must be in the sea, the underworld
Boyfriend:	i have no physical location i ws sent for u, and i have u ryt in my fingers you shall never escape
Christian Sister:	Him who baptizes with fire will roast u to ashes the fire of God will consume u
Boyfriend:	when time is gone it's time to go where time is endless
Christian Sister:	Jesus' blood wasn't wasted on Calvary
Boyfriend:	u don't have it with u
Christian Sister:	it's still very active today, i am covered by His blood
Boyfriend:	u have nothing but a loud mouth

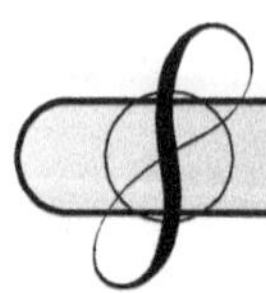

Christian Sister:	The Lord will protect me from every evil attack That's the scripture i gave u
Boyfriend:	that am about to shut at midnight tonight
Christian Sister:	The Lord rebukes u
Boyfriend:	damn!!
Christian Sister:	My God never goes to sleep neither does he slumber
Boyfriend:	see you tonight
Christian Sister:	His angels guard over me
Boyfriend:	i will put your faith to test
Christian Sister:	The Holy Ghost fire surrounds me
Boyfriend:	nothing don't be a FOOL
Christian Sister:	I knew u were the devil's agent
Boyfriend:	u will know me best tonight
Christian Sister:	You will know Jesus better
	The victory is mine but the battle is the Lord's. For he triumphed over u master by his death on the cross. Colossians 2:15
Boyfriend:	your blood smells nice gal

24

Christian Sister: Philippians 2:9-11

Boyfriend: Cannot wait to drain it all out am going to suck it right from your mouth like i have always done and my stuff u have in your tummy just proves to me i can have u whenever i want

Christian Sister: The Lord Jesus Christ is exalted in the highest place and has a name that is above every other name, at the mention of his name, every knee should bow and every tongue (including yours) confess that JESUS CHRIST IS LORD

Boyfriend: AM COMING FOR YOU RIGHT NOW

Christian Sister: For your own information, it's all flushed out by THE BLOODOF JESUS CHRIST. THE LORD WILL MEET U!

Boyfriend: (laughing) Please stop . . . (more laughing) I'm dying over here I KNEW IT U WERE JUST BEING A LOUD MOUTH

Christian Sister: NO! for your own information I MEANT EVERY WORD OF IT u shall eat your own flesh and drink your own blood Isaiah 49:26

Boyfriend:	(laughing) Please stop . . . (more laughing) I'm dying over here
Christian Sister:	i knew u were an agent of satan
Boyfriend:	AM INVITING YOU FOR DINNER AT MY HOUSE, BUZZ!!!
Christian Sister:	at the sea?
Boyfriend:	you coming? BUZZ!!!
Christian Sister:	Isaiah 1:18. The Lord is inviting u to His table
Boyfriend:	come we reason together. i know that and that's why am inviting you to my place tonight. coming?
Christian Sister:	am not a partaker of wickedness
Boyfriend:	don't be stupid BUZZ!!!
Christian Sister:	You know Jesus came to set captives like you free from that bondage
Boyfriend:	just answer my question BUZZ!!!
Boyfriend:	See ya, I gotta split

Christian Sister: I dine at the Lord's table light & darkness do not mix

Boyfriend: fine you can hang

Christian Sister: and the Lord Jesus Christ is waiting for u, with His arms out stretched. There is time for everything, and your time to be set free has come to give u peace, for He is the Prince of Peace Psalm 27:2 . . . When evil men advance against me to devour my flesh, When my enemies and my foes attack me they will stumble and fall that's what's going to happen to u

Boyfriend: you just full of illusions u need prayers divine intervention actually

Christian Sister: The WORD of God is living & active. Sharper than any double-aged sword, it penetrates even to dividing soul & spirit, joints & marrow, it judges the thoughts and attitudes of the heart. Hebrews 4:12 How does it feel, living your life knowing that u are headed for eternal damnation?

| *Boyfriend:* | what the f--k are u talking about, want to get on my nerves? |

Boyfriend has signed out (1/20/2009 3:38 PM)

< End of conversation >

What do you think?

Out of a needless desperation to be married, many believers have unwittingly taken the passenger seat as satanic agents drive the vehicle of their destiny furiously toward a cliff. Thank God this sister knows her scripture. But quoting scripture is not nearly enough at this stage. You can hear this strange boyfriend bragging and boasting that he has his deposits in her already.

By the way, I present my response to this brazen challenge from a satanic agent, and show how the Lord delivered her in a mere 14 days, in the very next chapter.

At this point let's pause to fire the following prayer arrow:

> *"Every power bragging and boasting against my God, receive divine judgment by fire in the name of Jesus."*

Is it not amazing that he is busy taunting and mocking her even as she hurls scripture after scripture at him?

Question: Why is this possible?

Answer: Satanic deposits. Evil plantations.
These invisible "strangers" are already
within.

Those who have spiritual eyes can sometimes see these evil deposits swimming around inside the body as serpents, fishes, stones. Meanwhile the victim continues on, unaware of their existence. In fact, some women have evil birds living in their womb right now, making such a womb barren or dead for all practical purposes. Such women urgently need to begin to fire this prayer bullet until victory is won:

> *"Every satanic plantation in my womb, come out now and burn to ashes in the mighty name of Jesus."*

For some people the plantations can be found not just inside but also outside. During hot prayer sessions, they can manifest as chains around the neck, or on the legs and hands, or as heavy loads upon the head. During His earthly ministry, the Lord Jesus could see these manifestations clearly. For instance, He could see the rope (chain) binding the woman in the following passage, while the religious leaders could not:

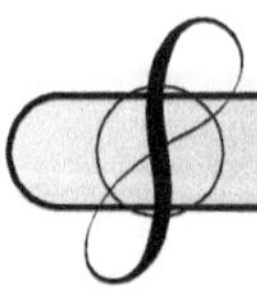

And he was teaching in one of the synagogues on the sabbath. And, behold, there was a woman which had a spirit of infirmity eighteen years, and was bowed together, and could in no wise lift up herself.

And when Jesus saw her, he called her to him, and said unto her, "Woman, thou art loosed from thine infirmity."

And he laid his hands on her: and immediately she was made straight, and glorified God.

And the ruler of the synagogue answered with indignation, because that Jesus had healed on the sabbath day, and said unto the people, "There are six days in which men ought to work: in them therefore come and be healed, and not on the sabbath day."

The Lord then answered him, and said, "Thou hypocrite, doth not each one of you on the sabbath loose his ox or his ass from the stall, and lead him away to watering?

And ought not this woman, being a daughter of Abraham, whom Satan hath bound, lo, these eighteen years, be loosed from this bond on the sabbath day?"

And when he had said these things, all his adversaries were ashamed: and all the people rejoiced for all the glorious things that were done by him.

Luke 13:10-17

The ability to see in the spirit is part of the package of nine gifts that the Holy Spirit delivers when you ask, seek, and knock persistently in prayer. The scripture calls this one *discernment* of spirit. It is the one indispensable gift with which those preparing themselves to be useful vessels in the kingdom of Christ must be equipped, otherwise satanic agents will be unrestricted, eating the flesh and drinking the blood of the very people to whom you are supposed to be ministering.

I must quickly add that the devil possesses a counterfeit of every gift offered by the Holy Spirit. This is why satanic agents can also speak in tongues and prophesy, and see "visions." I always feel concerned for those aimlessly looking for "prophets" to see visions for them, or psychics and astrologers to foretell their future. They are in mortal danger of getting more than they bargained for in the form of evil deposits, burdens, and yokes.

How do these evil plantations get into the body in the first place?

1. Through generational evil transfer.
2. Through sex with undercover satanic agents (in the dream or in the physical)
3. Through evil consumption (in the dream or in the physical)
4. Through prophecies given under satanic anointing

5. Evil transfer through kisses, touches, and other forms of satanic contact.
6. Sharing possessions with satanic agents (for example, clothes, bags, cosmetics).

In so many cases, these deposits can undergo a transformation once inside the body. They can transmute into lumps in the breast. In this particular case, the medical people will give it a name: breast cancer. If it settles in the brain, they call it brain tumor, and so on.

I am always speechless when I hear some believers claim (erroneously) that when they became born again, all those evil deposits disappeared because, according to them, old things are supposed to have passed away. Nothing can be further from the truth.

I know a sister who in the days of her ignorance and wanton lust for sex slept around and unfortunately contracted HIV. Now she is genuinely born again, loves the Lord and has fully committed her life to His service. But the demon of HIV is still there. It did not pack its evil baggage and leave once she gave her life to the Lord. She must live with the consequences of her past life, even though she is forgiven and on her way to heaven.

I know that the Lord can deliver her. But that is a subject for another day.

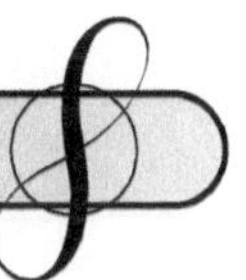

In the email conversation between our Christian sister and her boyfriend, she reels out scripture after scripture but her satanic boyfriend responds with laughter.

This is because he probably understands, as do most satanic agents, a key concept about spiritual authority. Here's how the scripture explains it:

> *(For the weapons of our warfare are not carnal, but mighty through God to the pulling down of strong holds;)*
>
> *Casting down imaginations, and every high thing that exalteth itself against the knowledge of God, and bringing into captivity every thought to the obedience of Christ;*
>
> *And having in a readiness to revenge all disobedience,* **when your obedience is fulfilled** *(emphasis mine).*
>
> *2 Cor 10:4-6*

This last sentence translates to:

The evil powers behind your troubles are not under any obligation to obey your voice when you are living in sin, even if you are just compromising your faith a little bit, in return for the fleeting pleasures of life.

To be clear, sin includes all the following (and more) according to this scripture in the book of Galatians:

> *"Now the works of the flesh are evident, which are: adultery, fornication, uncleanness, lewdness, idolatry, sorcery, hatred, contentions, jealousies, outbursts of wrath, selfish ambitions, dissensions, heresies, envy, murders, drunkenness, revelries, and the like; of which I tell you beforehand, just as I also told you in time past, that those who practice such things will not inherit the kingdom of God."*
>
> *Galatians 5:19-21*

According to the book of Revelation, it also includes:

> *"But the cowardly, unbelieving, abominable, murderers, sexually immoral, sorcerers, idolaters, and all liars shall have their part in the lake which burns with fire and brimstone, which is the second death."*
>
> *Rev 21:8*

True freedom begins with repentance from every known sin. Total freedom builds upon this foundation of repentance. To be victorious over the kind of stubborn problems that are assailing people from all spiritual and political persuasions, be they left, right, or center, you need to quickly build upon that foundation of repentance.

To do that you must:

1. Understand the time table of bondage—discover your "time of Jacob's trouble."
2. Learn the aggressive prayers of the rainmakers.

Armed with this new revelation about the timetable of bondage and how to deal with it decisively, you will be equipped to break fresh spiritual grounds in the days and weeks ahead.

Chapter Four

Conversations From Hell— Conclusion

Date: Thursday, January 22, 2009 at 9:41 PM

> *My Urgent Advice . . .*
>
> *Thank you for your emails and painstaking explanations. You made three fundamental mistakes:*
>
> *1. You disobeyed a man of God who has spiritual authority over you. In that case, God will not talk to you.*
>
> *2. You missed the clues the Holy Spirit was giving you. And they were many.*
>
> *3. From the emails, I gather you know the Lord. But because you are walking in disobedience, the enemy has been able to cast a strong witchcraft spell over you. That's why you are not alarmed about the mysterious nature of this "relationship."*

Right now, they are monitoring your life, day and night. And you placed yourself in that situation. In the spirit, it is as if you are engulfed in flames.

If you have to face this matter with the seriousness it deserves, you MUST start with a three-day Esther fast repenting before the Lord and asking Him for mercy. That's the time the Lord will give you the anointing to break this evil yoke. From now you cannot afford to joke with your midnight prayers.

I will need an update from you EXACTLY three days into your fasting. Then I'll tell you the next steps.

Without declaring a fast and following these instructions above, there is not much I can do to help. You are gone too deep for just ordinary prayers to be of any help.

Hoping to hear from you soon.

elisha

An Update

> *"To: 'elisha goodman'*
>
> *Date: Tuesday, February 3, 2009, 5:37 AM*
>
> *Hi elisha,*
>
> *I delayed in declaring a fast because i was on an Esther fast from the 9th–11th and from the 16th–18th of January and i was on partial (eating light meals thereafter) in between till the 25th, so i felt i needed energy to go on another Esther.*
>
> *Then I finally did go on an esther fast from saturday to monday, though i don't clearly remember my dreams but they had something to do with me holding a child, sometimes they looked like my children who have gone back to being a babies, and also i was flirting with a man, somebody i had an affair with in 2006/7, he was sipping red wine from the glass he held in his hands, while i had climbed a tree and behaving like a stripper. I had no underwear & i wanted him to notice but somebody called him and in frustration i went into the kitchen, trying to find something to cook. I remember holding something which looked like colorful vegetables (not green) which i was about to cut.*
>
> *Last week monday, two of my friends came over home, for a 14 day partial fast, just to stand with me in prayer. It has really been a great relief for me.*

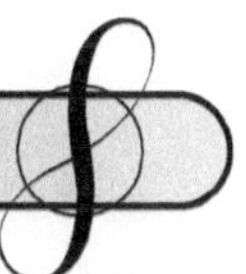

Ever since the revelations, i have had this strong desire to pray and plead for God's mercy over his life (as well as try to minister to him thru emails, if God gives him the grace to read them) and i have been searching the internet for information on satanism and what i came across really made me shiver and made me realise how serious this issue is, how careles i was to expose my babies to such a person, as well as how much God loves me to have preserved my life from destruction that i just broke down. Now am wondering if i should even bother about him at all.

When he used to say that every time he sat down and planned how our relationship would be, there was always some 'force' which frustrated his plans that he found himself making mistakes; i thought it was an evil force, now i realize it was the power of God protecting me. Then he would conclude by saying that he knew he was going to 'win.'

I really thank God for those ESF January prayer points, which by the grace of God i just decided to take seriously as i would include his name in place of my enemies, especially those addressing 'enemies of my marriage posing as friends to be exposed & be disgraced.' And God made him expose himself after the first Esther fast, and after the second one, he fully exposed himself when i broke the relationship.

I can't thank Him enough. Elisha i have proved these prayers really work, when taken seriously.

Please am ready for whatever am supposed to do next."

Then Finally, Great Deliverance 14 Days Later

Tuesday February 10, 2009 at 5:37 AM

Elisha,

Greetings in the name of our Lord.

I tried to send a detailed account of my deliverance last week but only to lose it when i was about to send. This is just a brief one.

I broke my Esther fast you had advised on monday midnight, last week. My two friends (i mentioned in the previous mail) continued the 14 day partial fast for me. I always joined at midnight to 3 AM or so.

Then on Wednesday midnight before 01:00 AM the Lord surprised us.

I was asleep on the couch in the living room as they were praying (in the same room). They woke me up after midnight. I said a few praise words to the Lord for a minute or 2 and then repentance for 2 or 3 mins, i was feeling sleepy so i got up and started praying in tongues for a while. The presence of God was so great that everyone was just in these powerful tongues when suddenly i found myself repeatedly saying

"IT IS FINISHED! IT IS FINISHED! SAYS THE LORD!"

40

In my heart i was saying "Lord, am i going to prophesy?" Then i continued again in such powerful tongues like never before that my friends held each of my hands. I was wondering why but we just continued. The next thing i fell down and my friends paused for a few seconds wondering why.

Then they drew closer to me and continued praying hard in tongues. Then demons started manifesting. I was fully aware of what was going on except that i wasn't in control of my body.

The demon started speaking through me, that they have defied all previous deliverance prayers, why were my friends so stubborn? He said he had been ordered to speak in a strange language (to him) so my friends could understand.

He also said the Lord Jesus Himself had actually come down, and His Angels were surrounding my house.

This demon revealed the following:

While my mum was expecting me, she had gone under the waters and offered me to them as their bride, i have been married to them even before i was born.

So they were in me with authority from my mother, they said, so that i should neither get married nor have children, "but her God helped her, she has children." And they have been chasing every man that got interested in me, including this one, cos i was already their wife.

From the time i was born, i have been living with them under the waters, i even had 3 kids there.

My own father's spirit also possessed me, he had locked my intelligence and vowed that i should never progress in life, "unless am not her real father."

My name was submitted under the waters, I was known to everyone underworld and they have been monitoring my life from my birth.

They were responsible for many illnesses in my life "but her God loves her so much that He always healed her miraculously they were behind the lower abdominal pains i have been experiencing for years."

As the demon mentioned these things, he was being commanded to remove whatever luggage they had brought in me. And then the demons started removing, pulling out, untying, undressing & cutting things, layers and layers of things i was literally wrapped into the hair on my head to my toe nails and throwing them away.

Every part / member of my body had several different things mounted on them. He lamented that they were just too many for him to remove as some things had sunk so deep into my flesh since they were put when i was still a baby.

But he was ordered to remove. He sunk my fingers into my skin to pull them out, others were being cut;

wedding rings & garments were taken off me

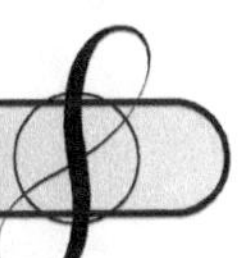

masks were removed from my face & the whole body

stickers on my forehead were removed

cosmetics

my lips were untied

the node in my brain that tied & locked my intelligence was cut

chains which had tied both my feet and hands were cut

snakes were pulled from my womb

Bras were removed

pants

beads rounds my waist

things tied on my reproductive organs

things around my arms, body, thighs, legs & feet were removed
spirit children were all being thrown away.

A week before i developed a small pimple like sore on my thigh. To my surprise it started spreading & spreading into something very big after squeezing it, which was very unusual.

This demon said, they were behind it, he had poked his finger on my thigh & inserted a snake, it wasn't just a normal abscess. Then he pulling it out, and for sure, when i woke up the following morning, the pain had greatly reduced & i squeezed out the pus.

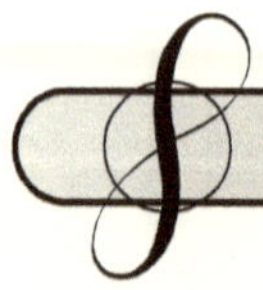

The demon cried foul as he finally left and vowed to go direct to my mother, that they were not going to leave her till she gives them another bride.

Afterwards, i just broke down as i felt so engulfed in God's love and mercy.

All i say was "Lord, in the assembly of men, i will declare your Name," and am writing a book about my life, up to my deliverance.

I have never written even an article but i know the Lord will give me the grace to write this book for His name's sake.

And i believe the Lord allowed me to hear everything for a purpose.

Your are free to share this testimony to the glory of God, just withhold my name.

God bless you.

Chapter Five

The Time of Jacob's Trouble

> *For thus saith the LORD; We have heard a voice of trembling, of fear, and not of peace.*
>
> *Ask ye now, and see whether a man doth travail with child? wherefore do I see every man with his hands on his loins, as a woman in travail, and all faces are turned into paleness?*
>
> *Alas! for that day is great, so that none is like it: it is even the time of Jacob's trouble; but he shall be saved out of it.*
>
> *For it shall come to pass in that day, saith the LORD of hosts, that I will break his yoke from off thy neck, and will burst thy bonds, and strangers shall no more serve themselves of him:*
>
> *Jer 30:5-8*

Understanding the Timetable of Bondage

We are now approaching the core of this presentation. What you are about to see in this chapter and in subsequent chapters is part of the spiritual arsenal that He has graciously revealed to us for our online ministry at *www.firesprings.com*.

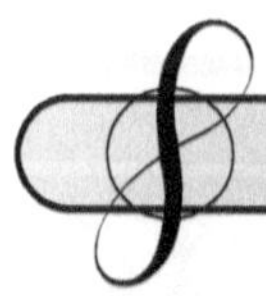

Diligent application of this principle is one of the reasons that you see so many praise reports on our websites daily. The Lord always confirms this teaching with signs and wonders in the lives of those He brings our way.

Praise the Lord.

Nicole's Story

Nicole was 37 years old. She was married for six years without a child and was becoming quite worried. At the promptings of a man of God whom the Lord had blessed with the gift of discernment, she began to ask questions.

Nicole's mother began to talk. And as she talked a pattern began to emerge. As it turned out, the mother had waited for ten years before she could have her first child (Nicole). She did not know Jesus as the savior at the time. She had no relationship with Him. In her desperation, she had visited all kinds of psychics and satanic prophets for a solution to her problem.

Typically, she would become pregnant, but after a few weeks something would happen. On those occasions, mysterious marks would appear on her body when she awoke. Or she would see red colors in her dream. Either way, the pregnancy was gone.

Finally, after ten years of running from one psychic "prophet" to another, Nicole was born. Family members thought her birth was unusual but they couldn't quite understand why.

Growing up, this child went through hell. Success and achievement escaped her, in spite of being both brilliant and exceptionally beautiful. In High School, she had a hard time making her grades. At university, it was a battle to graduate.

A day came however, when Nicole's fortunes began to change. After hearing a stirring message by a visiting Pentecostal preacher, her parents committed their lives to the Lord. She too became born again not long after that. As she began to study the scriptures and engage in the type of prayers I will introduce to you shortly, her life started to take on a new meaning. Through prayer and fasting, Nicole eventually was married at the age of thirty one.

Then the real battle began.

Immediately her husband became a target. Though a mature Christian, he was being bombarded by unusual problems from all sides. Without warning, he lost his high-flying job. He lost his beautiful home. All his well-connected friends disappeared.

Some years ago I got to know about the situation of this warm, Christian family. That was long before our website, *www.firesprings.com*, went live. We began to pray and to believe in the Lord for a turnaround breakthrough. After seven years, the Lord blessed this family with a beautiful baby girl.

But not all the problems went away. After the child was born, lack and poverty set in. As she was growing up, we began to notice certain disturbing patterns:

1. She was having problems in school.
2. No one seemed to like her.
3. She had no friends and often came home from school crying.

She changed schools but the problems persisted. The child was feeling rejection and was rapidly losing her self-esteem.

We were determined to get to the root of this matter. We launched a sustained campaign of aggressive prayer and fasting. It took time and many sleepless nights, but one day, the Lord answered us in His infinite mercies and revealed the secret of this long-running problem.

When He did, it took Him less than five minutes to hit the nail on the head.

An Amazing Discovery

I was in shock as the Lord began to unravel the mystery through scripture. He identified the powers behind the problem. He showed us how they operate. For the first time we understood why there was always a slight period of relief before the next major attack.

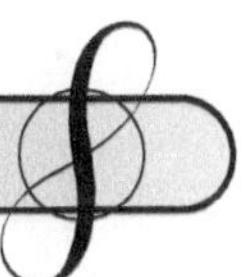

These cruel powers will allow their victims a brief respite. But surreptitiously, they will arrange for the person to make mistakes that will take them right back to square one. If they were starting to prosper, something will "happen" out of the blue and suddenly:

○ Prosperity stops, debt and poverty sets in
○ Helpers disappear
○ Marital distress begins

Again, after some time, the victim might succeed in climbing out of this cauldron of affliction. No problem. The powers will allow him or her to breathe some air of freedom, all the while preparing yet another time bomb to detonate in the future, bringing the individual crashing down to the bottom all over again.

And so the cycle continues. As these powers seek to regulate the lives of their victims and keep them at a certain level in life—the level at which the powers want them to remain.

Before I name names let's take a quick journey into scripture so we can establish a foundation for what I've presented thus far.

The Man Jacob and His Troubles

In the book of Genesis, we read about the unusual circumstances of Jacob's birth.

> *Now Isaac pleaded with the LORD for his wife, because she was barren; and the LORD granted his plea, and Rebekah his wife conceived. But the children struggled together within her; and she said, "If all is well, why am I like this?" So she went to inquire of the LORD.*
>
> *And the LORD said to her:*
>
> *"two nations are in your womb,*
> *two peoples shall be separated from your body;*
> *one people shall be stronger than the other,*
> *And the older shall serve the younger."*
>
> *So when her days were fulfilled for her to give birth, indeed there were twins in her womb. And the first came out red. He was like a hairy garment all over; so they called his name Esau. Afterward his brother came out, and his hand took hold of Esau's heel; so his name was called Jacob. Isaac was sixty years old when she bore them.*
>
> *Gen 25:21-26*

You may be tempted to conclude that Jacob's problems began while he was still in the womb. But there's more to it than that. His troubles actually happened in stages, beginning from before he was even conceived!

Jacob's Trouble: Act I

Let's step back one generation, to the time of Jacob's father, Isaac.

What was his birth like? You will recall that Isaac was the covenant child, promised of God to Father Abraham at an age when it was medically impossible for his wife, Sarah, to bear children.

As so often happens when we allow human calculations to interfere with God's divine purpose, this same Abraham, goaded by his wife Sarah, unwittingly opened a door for a satanic counterfeit to infiltrate his bloodline.

Let's pick up the narrative from the book of Genesis:

51

And Sarai Abram's wife took Hagar her maid the Egyptian, after Abram had dwelt ten years in the land of Canaan, and gave her to her husband Abram to be his wife.

And he went in unto Hagar, and she conceived: and when she saw that she had conceived, her mistress was despised in her eyes.

And Sarai said unto Abram, "My wrong be upon thee: I have given my maid into thy bosom; and when she saw that she had conceived, I was despised in her eyes: the LORD judge between me and thee."

Gen 16:3-5

What was the result of this? Before Isaac, the child of promise was even conceived, there was a formidable adversary on ground, ready to pounce when the time was right. No wonder we read this scripture a little while later:

> *And Abraham was a hundred years old, when his son Isaac was born unto him.*
>
> *And Sarah said, "God hath made me to laugh, so that all that hear will laugh with me."*
>
> *And she said, "Who would have said unto Abraham, that Sarah should have given children suck? For I have born him a son in his old age."*
>
> *And the child grew, and was weaned: and Abraham made a great feast the same day that Isaac was weaned.*
>
> *And Sarah saw the son of Hagar the Egyptian, which she had born unto Abraham, mocking.*
>
> *Gen 21:5-9*

Father Abraham made a costly mistake by listening to Sarah's advice to go into Hagar. Trying to help God in this manner is always a dangerous idea. The end product was Ishmael and we're still witnessing the effect of that mistake even today, in the never-ending drama unfolding in the Middle East.

Now watch this carefully. Abraham first introduced a spiritual counterfeit into his family line, and thus with his own hands opened the door to a group of powers to intimidate his family from generation to generation. I call these powers *The Intimidators*. According to the Bible account:

> *And Sarah saw the son of Hagar the Egyptian, which she had born unto Abraham, mocking.*
>
> *Wherefore she said unto Abraham, "Cast out this bondwoman and her son: for the son of this bondwoman shall not be heir with my son, even with Isaac."*
>
> *And the thing was very grievous in Abraham's sight because of his son.*
>
> *And God said unto Abraham, "Let it not be grievous in thy sight because of the lad, and because of thy bondwoman; in all that Sarah hath said unto thee, hearken unto her voice; for in Isaac shall thy seed be called.*
>
> *And also of the son of the bondwoman will I make a nation, because he is thy seed."*
>
> *Gen 21:9-13*

One simple mistake can give rise to powerful consequences that carry over from generation to generation.

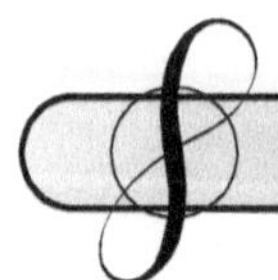

It is this type of spiritual carry-over that sets the stage for a person to be afflicted and mocked, and her break-throughs amputated anytime she attempts to claim God's divine blessings.

This is the problem of the intimidators in the spirit. They operate largely through what is known as *age group spirits*. These spirits are responsible for:

1. Satanic rivalry (between siblings and even between friends)
2. Leading people to a spiritual traffic jam, with no way out
3. Mocking spirits (they mock one's effort and prayers)
4. Expanding problems—making problems seem larger than they actually are.
5. Diverting destiny—they divert blessings and replace them with counterfeits.
6. Wasting lives and burying the potential of millions of people daily

Their primary assignment is to ensure that a person never progresses beyond a level set by satanic decree in the spirit. So long as one is ignorant of their activities, these powers will go underground and operate covertly, without being detected, using a weapon called the *satanic timer* to monitor and regulate the lives of their victims unhindered.

But the moment a child of God understands what's going on and begins to fight back with the appropriate spir-itual weapons that the Lord has provided in His word, then

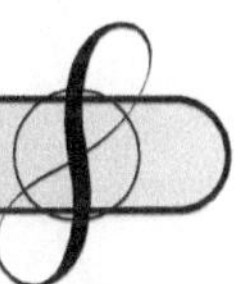

all hell could suddenly break loose, without any prior warning.

Here's where many people do the wrong thing. They become frightened and quit. However, rather than pulling back and running away, this is precisely the time to roll out the big guns, which you are going to see in this book shortly.

Jacob's Trouble: Act II

These powerful forces of intimidation have already been set in motion in a previous generation. In the generation of Jacob's father, their activities were manifested in the cruel mocking that Isaac received at the hands of Ishmael.

In Jacob's generation, these powers began to manifest right from the womb, in the form of a combat between him and his twin brother Esau. Jacob spent most of his adult life on the run. The intimidators, using their human agents, pursued him relentlessly. They pursued him to the point that he began to make mistakes. As I mentioned before, one of their strategies is to push people into making mistakes.

We must keep in mind that we are talking about spirits here. They are invisible to the naked eye. But in order to operate they must use human vehicles or agents. In Jacob's case, they used Esau to pursue him. This gave rise to one of the hottest prayer bullets we used to fire many years ago:

> *"Every spirit of Esau pursuing my destiny,*
> *fall down and die in the name of Jesus."*

What happened to Jacob? He ended up as a fugitive in a strange land, where he was later manipulated into marrying two sisters. These two wives came with extra baggage of their own, setting the scene for an epic rivalry, competition, and strife—the ideal atmosphere for the powers of intimidation to operate.

The man Jacob was left with the unenviable task of keeping the peace between four rival factions in one household, a nearly impossible task. One would think that because his two wives were sisters, there would be peace and harmony. No way!

This household was characterized by competition, envy, and jealousy:

> *And when Rachel saw that she bare Jacob no children, Rachel envied her sister; and said unto Jacob, "Give me children, or else I die."*
>
> *And Jacob's anger was kindled against Rachel: and he said, "Am I in God's stead, who hath withheld from thee the fruit of the womb?"*

> *And she said, "Behold my maid Bilhah, go in unto her; and she shall bear upon my knees that I may also have children by her."*
>
> *And she gave him Bilhah her handmaid to wife: and Jacob went in unto her.*
>
> *And Bilhah conceived, and bare Jacob a son.*
>
> *And Rachel said, "God hath judged me, and hath also heard my voice, and hath given me a son: therefore called she his name Dan."*
>
> *And Bilhah Rachel's maid conceived again, and bare Jacob a second son.*
>
> *And Rachel said, "With great wrestlings have I wrestled with my sister, and I have prevailed: and she called his name Naphtali."*
>
> *When Leah saw that she had left bearing, she took Zilpah her maid, and gave her Jacob to wife.*
>
> *Gen 30:1-9*

The intimidators thrive in an atmosphere of strife such as this. In this household, they eventually zeroed in on the star of the family, Joseph:

And when his brethren saw that their father loved him more than all his brethren, they hated him, and could not speak peaceably unto him.

And Joseph dreamed a dream, and he told it his brethren: and they hated him yet the more.

And he said unto them, "Hear, I pray you, this dream which I have dreamed:

For, behold, we were binding sheaves in the field, and, lo, my sheaf arose, and also stood upright; and, behold, your sheaves stood round about, and made obeisance to my sheaf."

And his brethren said to him, "Shalt thou indeed reign over us? Or shalt thou indeed have dominion over us?" And they hated him yet the more for his dreams, and for his words.

Gen 37:4-8

58

His brothers simply could not understand why Joseph was destined to rise above them. They wondered in resentment why he should be the most loved of their father. In the end, they were driven by hatred and anger to waste his life when an opportunity presented itself:

And when they saw him afar off, even before he came near unto them, they conspired against him to slay him.

And they said one to another, "Behold, this dreamer cometh. Come now therefore, and let us slay him, and cast him into some pit, and we will say, some evil beast hath devoured him: and we shall see what will become of his dreams."

And Reuben heard it, and he delivered him out of their hands; and said, "Let us not kill him."

And Reuben said unto them, "Shed no blood, but cast him into this pit that is in the wilderness, and lay no hand upon him, that he might rid him out of their hands, to deliver him to his father again."

And it came to pass, when Joseph was come unto his brethren, that they stript Joseph out of his coat, his coat of many colours that was on him;

And they took him, and cast him into a pit: and the pit was empty, there was no water in it.

And they sat down to eat bread: and they lifted up their eyes and looked, and, behold, a company of Ishmeelites came from Gilead with their camels bearing spicery and balm and myrrh, going to carry it down to Egypt.

> *And Judah said unto his brethren, "What profit is it if we slay our brother, and conceal his blood?*
>
> *Come, and let us sell him to the Ishmeelites, and let not our hand be upon him; for he is our brother and our flesh." And his brethren were content.*
>
> *Then there passed by Midianites merchantmen; and they drew and lifted up Joseph out of the pit, and sold Joseph to the Ishmeelites for twenty pieces of silver: and they brought Joseph into Egypt.*
>
> *Gen 37:18-28*

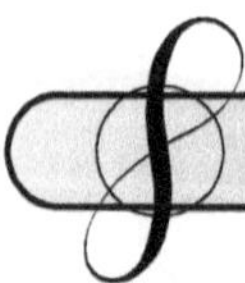

Jacob's Trouble: Act III

Well, they didn't quite succeed in destroying him. So they did the next best thing. They sold him into slavery in Egypt. But God was with Joseph and he ended up head of Potiphar's house. For a while, the intimidators pursuing his life allowed him a bit of relief while they regrouped to plan the next phase of their agenda.

Here's where you need to pause and take this prayer:

> *"Every evil agenda for my life, be scattered unto desolation in the name of Jesus."*

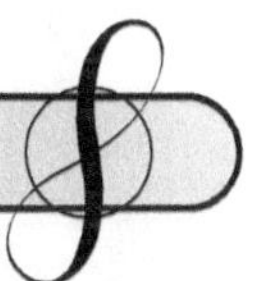

It wasn't long however, before the time table of bondage was re-activated, and without forewarning, Joseph found himself back in the furnace of affliction. This time they used the woman of the house. Here's what happened:

> *And it came to pass, as she spake to Joseph day by day, that he hearkened not unto her, to lie by her, or to be with her.*
>
> *And it came to pass about this time, that Joseph went into the house to do his business; and there was none of the men of the house there within.*
>
> *And she caught him by his garment, saying, "Lie with me:" and he left his garment in her hand, and fled, and got him out.*
>
> *And it came to pass, when she saw that he had left his garment in her hand, and was fled forth,*
>
> *That she called unto the men of her house, and spake unto them, saying, "See, he hath brought in a Hebrew unto us to mock us; he came in unto me to lie with me, and I cried with a loud voice:*
>
> *And it came to pass, when he heard that I lifted up my voice and cried, that he left his garment with me, and fled, and got him out. And she laid up his garment by her, until his lord came home."*
>
> *And she spake unto him according to these words, saying, "The Hebrew servant, which thou hast brought unto us, came in unto me to mock me:*

> *And it came to pass, as I lifted up my voice and cried, that he left his garment with me, and fled out."*
>
> *And it came to pass, when his master heard the words of his wife, which she spake unto him, saying, "After this manner did thy servant to me; that his wrath was kindled."*
>
> *And Joseph's master took him, and put him into the prison, a place where the king's prisoners were bound: and he was there in the prison.*
>
> *Gen 39:10-20*

Meanwhile, what was going on with his father Jacob?

> *And Jacob rent his clothes, and put sackcloth upon his loins, and mourned for his son many days.*
>
> *And all his sons and all his daughters rose up to comfort him; but he refused to be comforted; and he said, "For I will go down into the grave unto my son mourning."*
>
> *Thus his father wept for him.*
>
> *Gen 37:34-35*

You need to realize that in many cultures, the loss of children was considered a punishment worse than death itself. You see echoes of this when David's child with

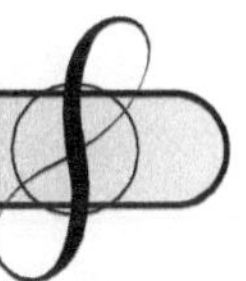

Bathsheba died and in the agony of Mary, mother of Jesus, when the Lord was crucified.

Here's how Jacob summarized his struggles in the furnace of affliction many years later when he stood before Pharaoh, king of Egypt in his old age.

> *And Pharaoh said unto Jacob, "How old art thou?"*
>
> *And Jacob said unto Pharaoh, "The days of the years of my pilgrimage are an hundred and thirty years: few and evil have the days of the years of my life been, and have not attained unto the days of the years of the life of my fathers in the days of their pilgrimage."*
>
> Gen 47:8-9

Many generations later, these powerful intimidating spirits were still at work in the lineage of Jacob. But now, let's fast-forward a few generations ahead.

Tracking Through the Ages

Was there a spiritual connection between the "mild" intimidation faced by Jacob's father (Isaac) and the full-blown persecution that Joseph, the beloved son, later suffered at the hands of his brothers? I believe so. If there was, can we pick up the thread in subsequent generations, following the biblical account? Yes, we can.

Let's now move beyond Isaac's generation, Jacob's generation, even Joseph's generation, to the household of a man called Elkanah in the book of 1 Samuel. This man is a descendant of Joseph.

> *Now there was a certain man of Ramathaim Zophim, of the mountains of Ephraim, and his name was Elkanah the son of Jeroham, the son of Elihu, the son of Tohu, the son of Zuph, an Ephraimite.*
>
> *1 Sam 1:1*

Did you notice it? He was from the house of Ephraim, the son of Joseph. This is the beginning of the popular story of Hannah, whose son, Samuel, was to become one of the greatest prophets Israel ever had. We are now approaching rainmaker territory here!

This godly woman was married to Elkanah, a direct descendant of Joseph, through Ephraim his second son. At this juncture you can see the thread linking the past with the present. No wonder the powers of the intimidators running along the family line were busy intimidating and harassing this woman, simply because she had no child.

To this very day, my eyes well up with tears every time I read this scripture. It is all too familiar. Let's follow the story:

> *And he had two wives; the name of the one was Hannah, and the name of the other Peninnah: and Peninnah had children, but Hannah had no children.*
>
> *And this man went up out of his city yearly to worship and to sacrifice unto the LORD of hosts in Shiloh. And the two sons of Eli, Hophni and Phinehas, the priests of the LORD, were there.*
>
> *And when the time was that Elkanah offered, he gave to Peninnah his wife, and to all her sons and her daughters, portions:*
>
> *But unto Hannah he gave a worthy portion; for he loved Hannah: but the LORD had shut up her womb.*
>
> *And her adversary also provoked her sore, for to make her fret, because the LORD had shut up her womb.*
>
> *And as he did so year by year, when she went up to the house of the LORD, so she provoked her; therefore she wept, and did not eat.*
>
> *1 Sam 1:2-7*

The keyword here is: Adversary. Her adversary did her best to intimidate Hannah. But this blessed woman was very wise. Instead of sitting complacently and complaining, she did what all spiritual eagles have done since the dawn of time. She took her case to the Lord in prayer.

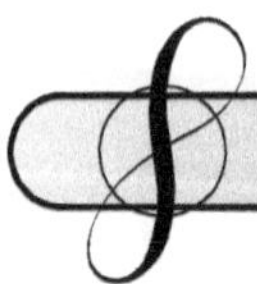

Let's slow down a bit to really study how this woman prayed. Here's the Bible's account:

> And she was in bitterness of soul, and prayed unto the LORD, and wept sore.
>
> And she vowed a vow, and said, "O LORD of hosts, if thou wilt indeed look on the affliction of thine handmaid, and remember me, and not forget thine handmaid, but wilt give unto thine handmaid a man child, then I will give him unto the LORD all the days of his life, and there shall no rasor come upon his head."
>
> And it came to pass, as she continued praying before the LORD, that Eli marked her mouth.
>
> Now Hannah, she spake in her heart; only her lips moved, but her voice was not heard: therefore Eli thought she had been drunken.
>
> And Eli said unto her, "How long wilt thou be drunken? put away thy wine from thee."
>
> And Hannah answered and said, "No, my lord, I am a woman of a sorrowful spirit: I have drunk neither wine nor strong drink, but have poured out my soul before the LORD.
>
> Count not thine handmaid for a daughter of Belial: for out of the abundance of my complaint and grief have I spoken hitherto."

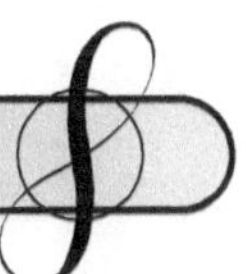

> *Then Eli answered and said, "Go in peace: and the God of Israel grant thee thy petition that thou hast asked of him."*
>
> *And she said, "Let thine handmaid find grace in thy sight." So the woman went her way, and did eat, and her countenance was no more sad.*
>
> *1 Sam 1:10-19*

The first thing you see here is that her prayer attracted immediate divine attention. The man of God, Eli, was quick to observe this woman agonizing in prayer, even though he mistakenly thought she was drunk. Why?

There's a level of prayer you attain at which it will appear as if you are crazy or drunk. There is no other explanation. This is the kind of prayer to pray when you want the hand of the devil to be removed from your life. It is a prayer of blood, sweat and tears. It is wrestling prayer. It is a prayer of conflict and confrontation; a make or break type of prayer that does not take "No" for an answer.

It is this type of prayer that "opens" the heavens and cause blessings to pour down like rain over God's people.

That was how Hannah was praying. Something *very* important happened here. She prayed and the man of God added his agreement. Ultimately, that's what sealed the matter—case closed.

> *"Again I say unto you, That if two of you shall agree on earth as touching any thing that they shall ask, it shall be done for them of my Father which is in heaven.*
>
> *For where two or three are gathered together in my name, there am I in the midst of them."*
>
> *Matt 18:19-20*

Do you now see why I do my best to urge, persuade, cajole, and provoke people into prayer? Thousands write to me every month asking me—a person they have never met—to pray for them. I always explain that they must learn to pray for themselves first. I can add my agreement certainly (if it's in line with the will of God) but they must do the "heavy lifting" themselves. Everyone must learn to travail for themselves and their loved ones in prayer. There's simply no way to get around it.

But do you know what? It is hard. Recently I met a man of God who is being used mightily in the healing ministry. He told me that when he is ministering in far-flung locations, the gift of healing in his life really flows like a river. But there is a problem. He finds it quite difficult to pray for himself. He was utterly shocked when I told him that I never allow anyone to pray for others (except when the Holy Spirit instructs otherwise) until they have prayed for themselves and have the results to show for it.

Back to Hannah.

She prayed and the Lord answered her. When her son Samuel was born, she did something mysterious. She took the child to the house of the Lord and handed him over to the Lord's service. Today, when we read this story, we may not even think of what could have happened to Samuel had he been left to grow up in the intimidating environment of his father's house.

Intimidation at Home

Through observation and revelation, we have come to understand that children growing up in households where spiritual intimidators are at work usually suffer some of the following:

1. Low self-esteem
2. Rejection and hatred
3. Bullying at school
4. Ridicule among their peers
5. Difficulty maintaining friends and relationships

All these traits end events were becoming manifest in the life of Nicole's daughter, the child she had in the seventh year of her marriage. The good news is that children like this are special. They are often chosen of God for a divine purpose. They have a great future and an awesome destiny, just like Isaac, Jacob, Joseph, and Samuel.

For sister Nicole's daughter, to obtain total freedom it has taken a continuous bombardment of prayer and patient counseling based on two key pieces of revelation. By the time the prayers got to a certain level, the spirits were forced to reveal themselves, according to the scripture:

> *"As soon as they hear of me, they shall obey me: the strangers shall submit themselves unto me.*
>
> *The strangers shall fade away, and be afraid out of their close places."*
>
> *Ps 18:44-45*

In time, the child began to speak up (or rather the spirits began to speak using her vocal cords). They were saying such things as:

○ My mom is a devil
○ I am a spirit from the waters
○ I cannot make it in life
○ This family will not profit me
○ I am going to die

She was seeing two places in the spirit: one was like a lake of fire and the other a very beautiful place. She would envision a huge, ugly creature trying to push her into the fire. But the Lord told us these were the strategies of the intimidators.

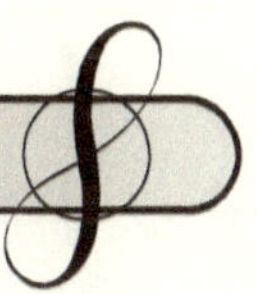

In this particular case they were working through two groups of spirits:

1. Spiritual age group
2. Strange children

What are these powers?

Spiritual Age Group

So far, we have been looking at the manifestation of these deadly powers of spiritual age group in the scripture. We have seen their wickedness against:

Isaac—They revealed themselves as mocking spirits (through Ishmael).

Jacob—They appeared as the spirit of the stubborn pursuer (through Esau).

Hannah—They posed as the household adversary.

These powers are still in operation today. In the life of Nicole's daughter, thanks to her grandmother, who opened the door in her days of ignorance without Christ, these stubborn, intimidating powers were hell bent on continuing their havoc, through the children at school and in the neighborhood.

Until Jesus said, "No."

Strange Children

More than once, the psalmist makes mention of this un-believably evil group while praying for his deliverance:

> *"Send thine hand from above; rid me, and deliver me out of great waters, from the hand of strange children;*
>
> *Whose mouth speaketh vanity, and their right hand is a right hand of falsehood."*
>
> Ps 144:7-8

When you talk about wickedness in the spirit realm, these take the Oscar. They are extremely ruthless and dangerous. They are totally committed to an evil agenda of stealing, killing, and destroying. They are on a permanent assignment to divert blessings and replace them with counterfeits. They have an urgent mandate to unleash catastrophe and desolation upon individuals, families, and nations without remedy.

Anytime you make the mistake of asking for blessing from the camp of the enemy, whether through consulting with psychics, fortune tellers, astrologers, satanic prophets posing as ministers of God, and so on, know that you are opening the door and inviting these wicked spirits into your life and family.

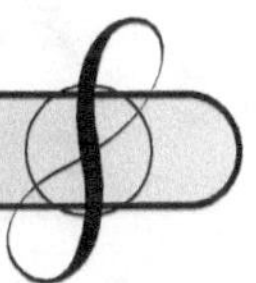

Whether you know it or not, ignorance is not an excuse in the spiritual realm. It doesn't matter that you didn't know what you were getting into. They will prove very stubborn to dislodge in the future. It's not hard for satanic agents to "bless" people with wealth, fame, and fortune.

What they are doing is nothing but a primitive trade by barter.

What they stole from others, they simply exchange for your divine virtues. And they do this without your knowledge. What they steal from you, they will barter in exchange for the virtues of their future victims. And yet they have a more insidious trick: all their so-called blessings come in bundles. This means they like to bundle sickness, incurable disease, accidents, and so many other forms of tragedy to people going to them to seek help.

As one man of God I know likes to say, "The devil has no free gifts." It is only the blessing of the Lord that makes us "rich and adds no sorrows," as the scripture has said. If God has mercy on you and opens your eyes a little bit to witness some of the transactions occurring in the spirit realm right now, you will take to your heels when "friends" try to invite you to go with them to satanic agents to solve your problems.

Here at *www.firesprings.com*, when we want people to see these spirits first-hand, we embed certain prayer bullets in their list of prayers. As they pray aggressively, over time the Lord will begin to show them things they would never have believed if someone were to tell them straightaway.

This is what happened to one of our new subscribers, Marilyn, a short while ago. Here, she recounts how recently, after serious prayers, she received a shocking revelation in a dream:

> *"Thank you for the prayer mentorship, my life is never the same. Though the battle gets tough at times—God is giving me the grace.*
>
> *Thanks to the multiple prayer points in all resources of the prayer academy, moreover to which the Holy Spirit is revealing a number of secret to my prayer life.*
>
> *I learned this one the hard way—after praying and trusting God amongst other things for a God fearing husband—I had expected answers promptly or even before I finish my prayers. But did the 14 days, the 21 days—the major breakthroughs in this area was deliverance from a number of strongholds, including self hatred, low self esteem, overeating (gluttony), spiritual spouses and marriages, etc.*
>
> *To me these are phenomenal breakthroughs, one will never appreciate being free until they know what it is to be free. While I was celebrating this—the spirit of despondency settled in—asking where is the husband . . . you are still wanting,*

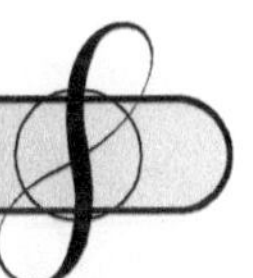

This lead to being seduced in the dream and had sex again, I was a bit perplexed over this re-occurring. The sex dream began when a co-worker who is espoused to marry in April, invited me to take a ride with him to go have some fun.

At first I declined the invitation in the name of wanting to get some rest, but finally got enticed. The car ride became a floating thing over the river in which a number of babies were floating too. At the end of this river was a coast side with sea or water creatures that I have not seen before. The tour guide in this dream was selling every creature as potential spouses to my wish, all I needed was to pick and choose—which I did in the dream. I woke up disappointed that this was happening to me and why was I not in my right minds to resist the devil in my dream.

It felt real, I prayed the reversal prayers to this bondage re-enforcing spirit, reversed any harm and infirmity transference. I went through my day partly fasting and praying and could not wait for my midnight warfare moment. As a direct consequence of the wet dream—a lustful spirit was released to my flesh—I had to hold myself and command the storm to be still.

At a midnight hour I prayed for deliverance from the evil transaction inflicted to my sexual organs through sex in the dream. This experience brought a loud-and-clear connection between sexual afflictions (for a lifetime I suffered hormonal

> *imbalances, ovarian cysts, uncontrollable lust that got me to masturbate even when I knew better not to because the Holy Ghost me warned me not to) and sex in the dream.*
>
> *Today sex in the dream does not represent fun (the devil sells that lie, only that this spiritual husbands come when one is unconscious—I had reached a point of hopelessness over my single hood) I thank God that I now have a glorious hope and I can overcome this element of bondage."*
>
> *New Subscriber Marilyn*

Wondering about the high rate of suicide among kids? Or the various atrocities we read about daily in articles with screaming headlines? Or the epidemic of sexual promiscuity and depravity that we are witnessing among teens today? Look no further.

Here are the hidden powers behind many of them. To deal with these problems permanently in your life and in your family, you must to be prepared to go far beyond the solutions offered by pop psychology and self-help apostles. You must get at the root of the problem. You must deal with these powers before they take advantage of the next crisis to release their deadly weapons.

There is no gentle way to deal with these spirits. There's an eye-opening encounter between these spirits (operating undercover, of course) and Elisha the prophet in the Bible. Let's read it together:

> *Then he went up from there to Bethel; and as he was going up the road, some youths came from the city and mocked him, and said to him, "Go up, you baldhead! Go up, you baldhead!"*
>
> *So he turned around and looked at them, and pronounced a curse on them in the name of the LORD. And two female bears came out of the woods and mauled forty-two of the youths.*
>
> *2 Kings 2:23-24*

Observe how they mocked the man of God? Elisha's aggressive response gives us a clue to the level of violence we must unleash against these deadly powers. Please keep this scripture in mind; we'll return to this later.

It is good to remember that we are in a spiritual war and our target is not the human vessels that we see but invisible spirits using these human surrogates to operate. Our prayers must be powerful enough to smoke them out and to deal a decisive blow on them once and for all. Before I introduce such prayers, I will first show you a most deadly weapon that these powers are using against individuals, families and even nations right now. They could even be using it against you as you read this.

Once you learn how to neutralize this ticking time bomb, your life, family and ministry will be sweeter than you ever imagined.

CHAPTER SIX

SECRET OF THE SPIRITUAL TIMER

To everything there is a season,
and a time to every purpose under the heaven . . .
Eccl 3:1

The stubborn powers we have been looking at operate very sophisticated timing devices. With them, they are able to regulate the lives of people, monitor their activities, and even increase the level of bondage from one generation to another.

Because they are so conscious of timing, when a payment falls due, they are sure to demand payment. Many believers today who come from a background of witchcraft and satanism are often left confused when some powers come to make aggressive demand for "payment" in the dream. In most cases, they have no understanding of the matter.

In some families people die mysteriously when they reach a certain age—40 is a favorite age. Often they die of the same disease that claimed either their parents or their siblings. Make no mistake about it: there is a price to pay for

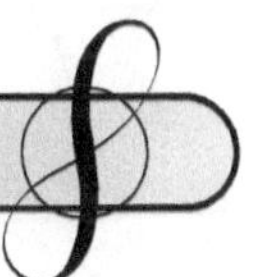

sin or ignorance, particularly when an individual enters into an evil agreement, knowingly or unknowingly, contrary to the commandments of the Lord.

All the wickedness we are seeing on the earth is already exacting a very heavy price. Some people are needlessly carrying the burdens of their evil ancestors without ever knowing it.

> *In those days they shall say no more:*
>
> *"The fathers have eaten sour grapes,*
> *And the children's teeth are set on edge."*
>
> *But everyone shall die for his own iniquity;*
> *every man who eats the sour grapes,*
> *his teeth shall be set on edge.*
>
> *Jer 31:29-30*

The result could manifest today as late marriages, barrenness, chronic poverty, divorce, rebellious children, hatred, suicidal tendencies, etc. The list goes on and on.

For many people the satanic clock started ticking the day they made a terrible mistake. For a particular Christian sister, a clock actually started ticking in the spirit realm the day she had an abortion. She often saw this clock in the dream, but she did not know what it was about.

For King David (in the Bible), it was the day he spied Bathsheba, the wife of Uriah the Hittite, bathing naked, at a time he should have been out leading the army of Israel into battle.

> *It happened in the spring of the year, at the time when kings go out to battle, that David sent Joab and his servants with him, and all Israel; and they destroyed the people of Ammon and besieged Rabbah. But David remained at Jerusalem.*
>
> *Then it happened one evening that David arose from his bed and walked on the roof of the King's house. And from the roof he saw a woman bathing, and the woman was very beautiful to behold.*
>
> *So David sent and inquired about the woman. And someone said, "Is this not Bathsheba, the daughter of Eliam, the wife of Uriah the Hittite?"*
>
> *Then David sent messengers, and took her; and she came to him, and he lay with her, for she was cleansed from her impurity; and she returned to her house.*
>
> *2 Sam 11:1-5*

When a spiritual timer has been set against an individual or family, it doesn't matter how high they rise in life. They will eventually fall from grace. It doesn't matter how successful they are today. All that they have managed to acquire will eventually develop wings and fly away.

It's dangerous for a clock to be ticking against a person when she does not even know it. For many people, it is a generational evil clock. Like the people in this passage here:

> *Now when the sun was going down, a deep sleep fell upon Abram; and behold, horror and great darkness fell upon him. Then He said to Abram: "Know certainly that your descendants will be strangers in a land that is not theirs, and will serve them, and they will afflict them four hundred years.*
>
> *And also the nation whom they serve, I will judge; afterward they shall come out with great possessions. Now as for you, you shall go to your fathers in peace; you shall be buried at a good old age.*
>
> *But in the fourth generation they shall return here, for the iniquity of the Amorites is not yet complete."*
>
> *Gen 15:12-16*

A timer had already been set to go off in the fourth generation. These people could have been flying high at the time this clock was being set against them in the spirit. No matter: as sure as night follows day, they were doomed to go into bondage in the fourth generation.

The reason these intimidators appear to be so powerful is because they operate a high-precision timer in the spirit realm. With this evil timer, they know exactly when to program a season of bondage into the lives of their victims. They know when to commit their victims to:

- The pit
- Slavery
- A cauldron of fire

To be quite frank, when a believer talks about going through a wilderness experience, the reality is that their lives have been programmed into one of these three things here. When you begin to notice that a life is prosperous today but poverty stricken tomorrow; in good health this week, but in hospital the next; today she is married, next day she's separated. This cycle continues to repeat and you can be sure there's a clock ticking against such individuals in the spirit. For such people to receive permanent victory, they urgently need to go to the Lord in prayer confessing their sins (and the sins of their ancestors).

That's the first step. The second step is to ask the LORD to show them the secret behind the problem. Finally, armed with this revelation, they should take up a lamentation like this:

> *"O Lord, let every satanic timer set against my destiny be scattered in the name of Jesus."*

Depending upon the level, it can take anywhere from a few days to many years of persistent, focused prayer for things to unravel. The Lord can do a progressive work, first by revealing the root causes, and after that, showing you the weapons and instruments used to keep the problem in place and to perpetuate it from one generation to the next.

To illustrate this point, let's return to the story of Nicole and her daughter. One night during prayer, the Lord showed us the satanic timer used against this child. It was a strange-looking, curiously shaped object, the size of a cell phone. The Lord instructed us to release divine thunder to shatter the device to irreparable pieces to prevent the problem from recurring.

And so we did. Oh, how we leapt at that prayer. From that day, this uniquely gifted child, who was prone to making silly mistakes in the past, was completely delivered.

To God be the glory, she has now claimed her rightful position as the head and not the tail in every activity she participates in.

Once a timer has been set against a person in the spirit, she or he will be under continuous surveillance. There's often a period of false calm while all the powers assigned to the case await some sort of crisis to trigger a full-scale attack. Once the ball has been set rolling, then things can truly get out of hand.

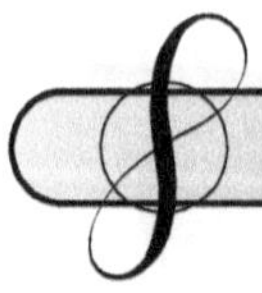

The Weapon of Shock

Let's briefly go back to the book of Job to review how a seed planted in the spirit can introduce terrible problems into the lives of individuals, families, and even nations here on earth.

> *And the LORD said unto Satan, "Hast thou considered my servant Job, that there is none like him in the earth, a perfect and an upright man, one that feareth God, and escheweth evil?"*
>
> *Then Satan answered the LORD, and said, "Doth Job fear God for nought?*
>
> *Hast not thou made an hedge about him, and about his house, and about all that he hath on every side? thou hast blessed the work of his hands, and his substance is increased in the land.*
>
> *But put forth thine hand now, and touch all that he hath, and he will curse thee to thy face."*
>
> *And the LORD said unto Satan, "Behold, all that he hath is in thy power; only upon himself put not forth thine hand." So Satan went forth from the presence of the LORD.*
>
> *And there was a day when his sons and his daughters were eating and drinking wine in their eldest brother's house:*
>
> *And there came a messenger unto Job, and said, "The oxen were plowing, and the asses feeding beside them:*

84

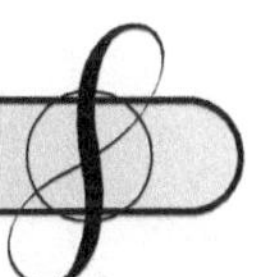

And the Sabeans fell upon them, and took them away; yea, they have slain the servants with the edge of the sword; and I only am escaped alone to tell thee."

While he was yet speaking, there came also another, and said, "The fire of God is fallen from heaven, and hath burned up the sheep, and the servants, and consumed them; and I only am escaped alone to tell thee."

While he was yet speaking, there came also another, and said, "The Chaldeans made out three bands, and fell upon the camels, and have carried them away, yea, and slain the servants with the edge of the sword; and I only am escaped alone to tell thee."

While he was yet speaking, there came also another, and said, "Thy sons and thy daughters were eating and drinking wine in their eldest brother's house:

And, behold, there came a great wind from the wilderness, and smote the four corners of the house, and it fell upon the young men, and they are dead; and I only am escaped alone to tell thee."

Then Job arose, and rent his mantle, and shaved his head, and fell down upon the ground, and worshipped,

And said, "Naked came I out of my mother's womb, and naked shall I return thither: the LORD gave, and the LORD hath taken away; blessed be the name of the LORD."

In all this Job sinned not, nor charged God foolishly.

Job 1:8-2:1

From the day a simple conversation concerning Job's life took place in the heavenly realm, a clock began to tick.

Tick-tock . . . tick-tock . . . tick-tock.

No one could have imagined the scale of devastation that satan was planning to unleash against this righteous man. The campaign of terror against him is best understood by applying what is known in the world of politics and economics as the crisis theory of change or the *shock doctrine*.

In its simplest form, shock doctrine states that only a massive crisis—actual or perceived—produces real change. It holds that when a crisis strikes (and people are still reeling from the shock) there's a small window of opportunity, and one can take advantage of the confusion and chaos to achieve permanent change.

To ensure lasting success, so the theory goes, one should use a "blitzkrieg" approach to unleash change suddenly and quickly in such a way that resistance would be impossible. In other words, surround your victims in a "fog of transition" while the changes are being made, and they won't have a chance to organize or protect themselves while the ground is shifting under their feet.

Talk about satanic ambush! In Job's situation, the enemy unleashed wave upon wave of devastation to try to change his belief and accept to curse God to his face. It didn't work. He then switched tactics, this time using human

proxies, beginning with his wife, to pressure him into turning his back on God. Again it failed.

In our modern world, the devil sometimes manufactures a problem, then sends in his foot soldiers (unsurrendered believers, friends, and family) to go in and persuade the victim to accept what she would not ordinarily think of doing.

I know many Christian sisters who were persuaded by "friends" to visit psychics, fortunetellers, sorcerers—simply because they were in a hurry to get married.

Today the marriage is no more. One thing many people fail to realize is that the enemy can take advantage of any situation to create a crisis in order to form covenants with them, and later transfer this evil covenant to generations yet unborn.

This is a hidden spiritual truth.

From emails I receive daily, it is clear to me that the powers of darkness can unleash a flood of affliction on their victim or a member of their family. Later, they will send their agent (posing as a Christian friend or concerned relative) to persuade them to go see a traditional healer or a New Age practitioner, who is nothing more than a glorified shop front for the devil.

When out of ignorance a person takes the bait, they soon discover that the sickness could indeed disappear, but only to be replaced by something even more deadly. This is satanic exchange at work: what they couldn't maneuver their victim to do in the past, with a sudden and life-threatening crisis, it is possible to manipulate them to swallow the bitter medicine, almost at gun point.

This is called spiritual shock therapy. In economics it is called *economic shock therapy*. Many economists believe this kind of shock therapy has been applied for decades against developing nations by the Bretton Woods institutions, popularly known as the World Bank and the International Monetary Fund (IMF). Their "solutions" always leave a trail of carnage and devastation wherever they've been implemented.

For instance, the kind of economic shock therapy that the IMF administers to poor nations has sometimes been blamed for helping to transfer massive public wealth into the hands of a few private corporations or individuals, right *after* a crisis, such as an earthquake, flood, tsunami, etc. has occurred.

Many economists and other experts now believe that the IMF strategy has been responsible for exacerbating poverty in most of the third world today, while at the same time engineering the greatest transfer of wealth from the public domain into the pockets of private individuals and corporations in decades.

Perhaps the IMF should be renamed the *International Merchant of Famine*. What the IMF does in the natural realm, some entities also do covertly in the spiritual realm. These invisible powers apply shock therapy in the form of debt, sickness, and turbulence to unsuspecting people every night while they are fast asleep.

The point of shock therapy is to open up an individual, family, or nation for their potentials to be harvested and traded out in the spirit realm, with or without their consent. The scripture has given us a clue as to the identity of these powers:

> *Woe to the bloody city! It is all full of lies and robbery; the prey departeth not;*
>
> *The noise of a whip, and the noise of the rattling of the wheels, and of the pransing horses, and of the jumping chariots.*
>
> *The horseman lifteth up both the bright sword and the glittering spear: and there is a multitude of slain, and a great number of carcases; and there is none end of their corpses; they stumble upon their corpses:*
>
> *Because of the multitude of the whoredoms of the well favoured harlot, the mistress of witchcrafts, that sells nations through her whoredoms, and families through her witchcrafts (emphasis added).*
>
> *Nah 3:1-4*

Of late, the high priestess of economic witchcraft has been busy creating shockwaves and turbulence in the global economy. Together with their agents in the secular media, she is moving aggressively to usher in a new era of:

- One world under debt
- One world under fear
- One world under shock

It is important to note that anyone who is under any kind of consumer debt, such as credit cards—and even mortgage debt—has willingly handed over their economic future to this mistress of witchcrafts identified in the scripture we just read, whether they are aware of it or not.

Let's return to the case of Job. No amount of crisis or devastation could quite push this righteous man to turn his back on his God. We need to learn from this. We should never allow crisis, no matter how severe, to shift our faith and focus from the Lord.

Like Hannah, we should look for an opportunity to pray long and hard when we are faced with crisis. The powers fighting believers day and night use spiritual timers to program and execute their evil agenda. If they cannot precipitate a crisis, they will lie in wait patiently for one to occur naturally. Then they will pounce.

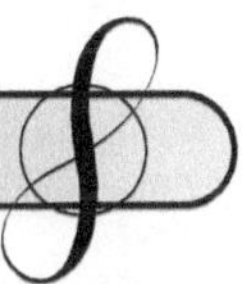

Warning: Danger Ahead!

This is one of the reasons I strongly advise that you should not jump from pillar to post, or from pastor to pastor, seeking for people to pray for you in times of crisis. There is a better way, which you are going to discover in the next chapter.

Many people in crisis are unaware that there are satanic agents all around, waiting with open arms for them to walk into their trap. Some of these agents can be difficult to spot, because they sometimes masquerade as ministers of light, but inwardly they are ravenous wolves. They are just waiting for people when they are most vulnerable—at the time of crisis.

These days, they are all over the Internet. You must be careful out there. It is becoming very, very dangerous. So what should you do in the midst of crisis and shock? I am glad you asked. Just turn the next page and you'll see.

Chapter Seven

Crisis Prayers of the Rainmakers

> *"Fear not, O land; be glad and rejoice: for the LORD will do great things.*
>
> *Be not afraid, ye beasts of the field: for the pastures of the wilderness do spring, for the tree beareth her fruit, the fig tree and the vine do yield their strength.*
>
> *Be glad then, ye children of Zion, and rejoice in the LORD your God: for He hath given you the former rain moderately, and he will cause to come down for you the rain, the former rain, and the latter rain in the first month.*
>
> *And the floors shall be full of wheat, and the fats shall overflow with wine and oil.*
>
> *And I will restore to you the years that the locust hath eaten, the cankerworm, and the caterpiller, and the palmerworm, my great army which I sent among you.*

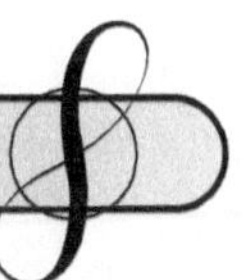

> *And ye shall eat in plenty, and be satisfied, and praise the name of the LORD your God, that hath dealt wondrously with you: and my people shall never be ashamed."*
>
> *Joel 2:21-26*

The scripture is full of examples of men and women who had reached the end of the road. Then they came to the realization that they needed a divine intervention before they could move forward. And they needed it immediately—not next year; not next week; not even tomorrow. They needed it now.

> *"Hide not thy face from me in the day when I am in trouble; incline thine ear unto me: in the day when I call answer me speedily."*
>
> *Ps 102:2*

Many times the Lord does answer immediately. while the answer could take some time to manifest in the physical realm for you to see. Instant answer, progressive results, such as in this case:

> *And as he entered into a certain village, there met him ten men that were lepers, which stood afar off:*
>
> *And they lifted up their voices, and said, "Jesus, Master, have mercy on us."*
>
> *And when he saw them, he said unto them, "Go shew yourselves unto the priests." And it came to pass, that, as they went, they were cleansed.*
>
> *And one of them, when he saw that he was healed, turned back, and with a loud voice glorified God,*
>
> *And fell down on his face at his feet, giving him thanks: and he was a Samaritan.*
>
> *Luke 17:12-16*

Other times, the prayer and the answer can occur nearly instantaneously, with little or no breathing space at all:

> *And it came to pass at the time of the offering of the evening sacrifice, that Elijah the prophet came near, and said, "LORD God of Abraham, Isaac, and of Israel, let it be known this day that thou art God in Israel, and that I am thy servant, and that I have done all these things at thy word.*

> *Hear me, O LORD, hear me, that this people may know that thou art the LORD God, and that thou hast turned their heart back again."*
>
> *Then the fire of the LORD fell, and consumed the burnt sacrifice, and the wood, and the stones, and the dust, and licked up the water that was in the trench.*
>
> *1 Kings 18:36-38*

Here's a landmark example:

> *And they came to Jericho: and as he went out of Jericho with his disciples and a great number of people, blind Bartimaeus, the son of Timaeus, sat by the highway side begging.*
>
> *And when he heard that it was Jesus of Nazareth, he began to cry out, and say, "Jesus, thou Son of David, have mercy on me."*
>
> *And many charged him that he should hold his peace: but he cried the more a great deal, "Thou Son of David, have mercy on me."*
>
> *And Jesus stood still, and commanded him to be called. And they call the blind man, saying unto him, "Be of good comfort, rise; he calleth thee."*
>
> *And he, casting away his garment, rose, and came to Jesus.*

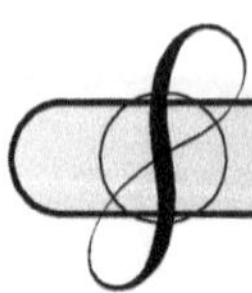

> *And Jesus answered and said unto him, "What wilt thou that I should do unto thee?" The blind man said unto him, "Lord, that I might receive my sight."*
>
> *And Jesus said unto him, "Go thy way; thy faith hath made thee whole. And immediately he received his sight, and followed Jesus in the way."*
>
> *Mark 10:46-52*

Now we are going to look at a class of people who moved in such a realm of prayer. I've decided to call them *the rainmakers*, for lack of a better term.

What is rain? In the scripture, rain symbolizes divine blessings, favor, power, and anointing. You see this clearly in the opening scripture from the book of Joel:

> *"Be glad then, ye children of Zion, and rejoice in the Lord your God; for He hath given you the former rain moderately, and He will cause to come down for you the rain, the former rain, and the latter rain in the first month.*
>
> *. . .*

> *And it shall come to pass afterward, that I will pour out my spirit upon all flesh; and your sons and your daughters shall prophesy, your old men shall dream dreams, your young men shall see visions:*
>
> *And also upon the servants and upon the handmaids in those days will I pour out my spirit."*
>
> *Joel 2:23, 28-29*

Let's begin by looking at a very popular rainmaking event in the Bible.

Rainmaker #1: Elijah Prays to Cancel a Decree

> *And Elijah said unto Ahab, "Get thee up, eat and drink; for there is a sound of abundance of rain."*
>
> *So Ahab went up to eat and to drink. And Elijah went up to the top of Carmel; and he cast himself down upon the earth, and put his face between his knees,*
>
> *And said to his servant, "Go up now, look toward the sea." And he went up, and looked, and said, "There is nothing." And he said, "Go again seven times."*

> *And it came to pass at the seventh time, that he said, "Behold, there ariseth a little cloud out of the sea, like a man's hand." And he said, "Go up, say unto Ahab, Prepare thy chariot, and get thee down, that the rain stop thee not."*
>
> *And it came to pass in the mean while, that the heaven was black with clouds and wind, and there was a great rain. And Ahab rode, and went to Jezreel.*
>
> *1 Kings 18:41-45*

This passage has always amazed me. A great man once said that a problem cannot be solved with the same level of awareness and knowledge that created it. To which we may also add that a crisis cannot be resolved with the same level of anointing that created it. It will take a higher anointing to uproot the problems staring many believers in the face today.

In this passage, we see Elijah, a highly anointed prophet of the Most High, praying for rain after three-and-a-half years of drought. Recall that he was the one who decreed this drought into the land as punishment for the wickedness of the people.

At the time he issued his powerful decree, it only took him a few sentences and the deed was done. But three and half years later, when it came time to reverse the decree,

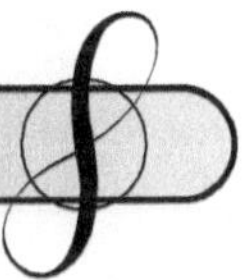

he had to engage in an aggressive form of prayer before anything could happen at all. Not once. Not twice. But seven times.

Please catch a revelation here. The Bible often talks about a seven-fold restoration, as in this scripture:

> *Men do not despise a thief, if he steals to satisfy his soul when he is hungry;*
>
> *But if he be found, he shall restore sevenfold; he shall give all the substance of his house.*
>
> *Prov 6:30-31*

We should realize of course that when the scripture speaks about this type of restoration, what is also implicit in such a statement is that it will require a seven-fold anointing to get the job done.

Like this interesting case of Elijah.

What do you imagine he was doing with his head between his knees those seven consecutive times? Praying, revoking the previous decree that had gone forth; filing a counter report in the heavens. That's what he was doing. This happened in the Old Testament.

In the New Testament book of James, the writer really pulled back the curtains to give us a glimpse of what happened back then. Let's read the passage:

> *Elias was a man subject to like passions as we are, and he prayed earnestly that it might not rain: and it rained not on the earth by the space of three years and six months.*
>
> *And he prayed again, and the heaven gave rain, and the earth brought forth her fruit.*
>
> *James 5:17-18*

The first statement I want to make about the prayer of the rainmakers is this:

> **Golden Statement 1:**
>
> *You must be prepared to confront every crisis at a level of anointing higher than the level that created it.*

For example, if someone placed a curse of sickness, barrenness, or poverty upon your family line, and as a result the whole family is laboring under the yoke of evil patterns such as cancer or divorce, you will need to operate from a level higher than that satanic anointing in order to destroy the problem from the root.

This is a very serious matter we are discussing here. One prayer warrior I know was waiting at a bus shelter this past week when a satanic agent came up behind her and began to issue incantations. This sister had no idea what was going on behind her back until the Holy Spirit quickened her to turn around. She turned and to her surprise this strange woman was gazing directly at the sun, mumbling incantations, with one hand pointed at her. The prayer warrior had never met this person before.

Immediately she jumped to her feet, as the Holy Ghost began to drop some "bullets" in her spirit, such as this one:

> *"Every power facing the sun against my life,*
> *fall down and die in the name of Jesus."*

Notice the prayer did not say "person." It was targeted directly at the unseen powers using this woman for an evil purpose. When the "bullet" hit home, the satanic agent had no option but to flee. (You should be aware that this incident did not happen in some African country. It happened right here in Canada, in the city where I live. It is the manifestation of the spirit of international witchcraft.) But it is not every time that the agent can escape this type of powerful head-to-head encounter unscathed. There are times when the Lord may decide to deal with both the horse and its rider:

> *Then sang Moses and the children of Israel this song unto the LORD, and spake, saying, "I will sing unto the LORD, for he hath triumphed gloriously: the horse and his rider hath he thrown into the sea."*
>
> *Exodus 15:1*

Earlier on, we witnessed how the youths mocking Elisha the prophet could not escape divine judgment for allowing some wicked powers to use them against one of the most powerful generals in the Lord's army. That was an unusual display of anointing. To get to this realm does not happen by chance or accident. You cannot contact it simply by watching a famous minister on television and claiming his anointing. No one will ever transfer this type of anointing to you, except under very rare, very special circumstances.

Remember how Elisha received his anointing. Even his master Elijah had to go through a prolonged season of preparation before he could perform at this championship level. Here's how one passage describes it:

> *And the angel of the LORD came again the second time, and touched him, and said, "Arise and eat; because the journey is too great for thee."*

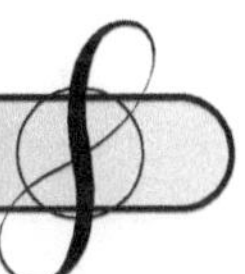

> *And he arose, and did eat and drink, and went in the strength of that meat forty days and forty nights unto Horeb the mount of God.*
>
> *1 Kings 19:7-8*

It saddens me when I see some believers who have been led to believe they can contact anointing from ministers of God the easy way, without having to crucify their flesh, carry their cross daily, and follow Jesus.

Sure they may end up "tasting" a little bit of it, but you can be sure anointing of this sort won't be sufficient when the prophets of Baal appear and ask, "Where is your God?" In fact it may not even be sufficient to retain divine blessings for any amount of time.

There is a price to pay for anointing and spiritual power. It is not free (only salvation is free). It is a heavy price and few are prepared to pay it (please understand that I'm not talking about money here). This is the reason we are witnessing so much powerlessness, frustration, and hopelessness in the body of Christ today. Many people are not ready to pay the price.

Before we go to the next section, here's another great example. This one should convince you that there's an urgent need to begin to operate at a higher level of anointing. You

will need to if you want to reverse evil decrees against your life and family. First, let's see how things went wrong for an entire city and how the problem was solved many centuries later:

> Then Joshua charged them at that time, saying, "Cursed be the man before the LORD who rises up and builds this city Jericho; he shall lay its foundation with his firstborn, and with his youngest he shall set up its gates."
>
> *Josh 6:26*

Did this ever come to pass?

> In his days did Hiel the Bethelite build Jericho: he laid the foundation thereof in Abiram his firstborn, and set up the gates thereof in his youngest son Segub, according to the word of the LORD, which he spake by Joshua the son of Nun.
>
> *1 Kings 16:34*

But that was not the end of the matter. For hundreds of years, there was serious crisis in this city because of this decree in the spirit. Fortunately, someone came along with a double anointing upon his life and put an end to the devastation permanently.

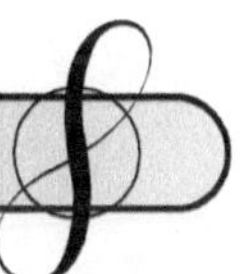

> *And the men of the city said unto Elisha, "Behold, I pray thee, the situation of this city is pleasant, as my lord seeth: but the water is naught, and the ground barren."*
>
> *And he said, "Bring me a new cruse, and put salt therein." And they brought it to him.*
>
> *And he went forth unto the spring of the waters, and cast the salt in there, and said, "Thus saith the LORD, I have healed these waters; there shall not be from thence any more death or barren land."*
>
> *So the waters were healed unto this day, according to the saying of Elisha which he spake.*
>
> *2 Kings 2:19-22*

Rainmaker #2: Hannah's Secret Weapon

Many people write to me saying they are not able to pray with holy aggression for one reason or another. Sometimes this can be due to the constraints imposed by where they live. They are concerned about making too much noise and distracting other occupants of the house at the midnight hour.

Others feel they can just pray at heart and it will still get the job done.

Well, let's look in the scriptures and see how Hannah did it. Obviously, in her situation, considering the hallowed surroundings of the temple of God, she dared not pray at the top of her voice. But she still prayed aggressively to the extent that the man of God noticed her facial contortions, which were borne out of the fiery intensity of her deeply distressed soul.

She was praying from the depths of her being.

Let's look at this again:

> *And it came to pass, as she continued praying before the LORD, that Eli marked her mouth.*
>
> *Now Hannah, she spake in her heart; only her lips moved, but her voice was not heard: therefore Eli thought she had been drunken.*
>
> *And Eli said unto her, "How long wilt thou be drunken? put away thy wine from thee."*
>
> *And Hannah answered and said, "No, my lord, I am a woman of a sorrowful spirit: I have drunk neither wine nor strong drink, but have poured out my soul before the LORD."*
>
> *1 Sam 1:12-15*

I can imagine tears rolling down her cheeks as she poured out her soul to God. What happened? The Lord granted her the desire of her heart. I often say that when you learn to really pray (to the level of breakthroughs) over your situation, others you don't even know will be compelled by the spirit of God to add their agreement and stand in the gap for you.

This is entirely different from the usual practice of believers who have learned the bad habit of firing off prayer requests to hundreds of places, without ever taking the time to pray long and hard over their problems first. There is a deep secret revealed by this one incident in the Bible. This leads us to:

> **Golden Statement 2:**
>
> *The Lord will never ignore the tears of His praying saints.*

In fact, tears take on a special significance before God when mingled with the fire of aggressive prayer. The Lord preserves those tears and even converts them to a weapon of war in the spirit.

> *"You number my wanderings;*
> *Put my tears into Your bottle;*
> *Are they not in Your book?*
> *When I cry out to You,*
> *Then my enemies will turn back;*
> *This I know, because God is for me."*
>
> *Ps 56:8-9*

Personally, when I need to bully the bullies and cause serious damage in the camp of the enemy, this has always been my weapon of choice. There's a big mystery attached to this. Holy tears can touch the very heart of God. Here's how He states it:

> *Thus saith the LORD, "The God of David thy father, I have heard thy prayer, I have seen thy tears: behold, I will heal thee:"*
>
> *2 Kings 20:5*
>
> *Let the priests, the ministers of the LORD, weep between the porch and the altar, and let them say, "Spare thy people, O LORD, and give not thine heritage to reproach, that the heathen should rule over them: wherefore should they say among the people, Where is their God?"*

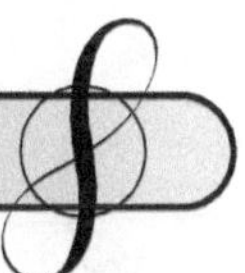

> *Then will the LORD be jealous for his land, and pity his people.*
>
> *Yea, the LORD will answer and say unto his people, "Behold, I will send you corn, and wine, and oil, and ye shall be satisfied therewith: and I will no more make you a reproach among the heathen:"*
>
> *Joel 2:17-19*

If the Holy Spirit ever lays a burden on your heart and you can persist in prayer until the tears suddenly begin flowing freely down your face like a stream of water, know for a truth that you have touched the heart of God.

At that level anything can happen. What the Lord might tell you to do may very well sound crazy to those who have never entered into this realm of prayer. I remember a time of great distress in my life many years ago. My entire world came crashing down in a matter of hours. What took me years to build simply evaporated in the blink of an eye. I had no more strength left in me—or so I thought.

I didn't know when I started praying, but suddenly, without any warning, the tears began flowing uncontrollably. This startled me, as I am not one given to emotional displays or sentimentality. Then I heard the voice of the Holy Spirit very clearly, giving me precise instructions on what to do. Within 72 hours of diligently carrying out the

instructions to the letter, there was a powerful shift in the spirit. All the satanic armies around me were scattered.

Following this power encounter was double divine restoration of all that I'd lost to the enemy.

This is strong stuff, not theory or theology. You will soon have an opportunity to put these principles to the test, should you choose to. The Lord Jesus was operating in an unusual realm of prayer at Gethsemane. The Bible describes this epic scene in the book of Hebrews:

> *Who in the days of his flesh, when he had offered up prayers and supplications with strong crying and tears unto him that was able to save him from death, and was heard in that he feared;*
>
> *Heb 5:7*

Did you see it? *"Prayers and supplications with strong crying and tears . . ."*

This is the crisis prayer of the rainmakers in its finest form. It is the essence of the other type of prayer that Jesus taught but almost no one talks about. Truly this is a divinely approved response in the time of crisis. I just can't resist giving you just one more powerful example. This time we journey to the book of Luke, to the story of Mary and Martha, the sisters of Lazarus.

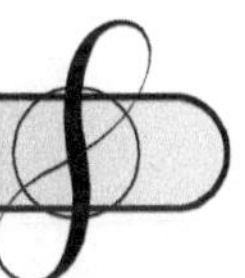

> *Then when Mary was come where Jesus was, and saw him, she fell down at his feet, saying unto him, "Lord, if thou hadst been here, my brother had not died."*
>
> *When Jesus therefore saw her weeping, and the Jews also weeping which came with her, he groaned in the spirit, and was troubled,*
>
> *And said, "Where have ye laid him?" They said unto him, "Lord, come and see."*
>
> *Jesus wept.*
>
> *John 11:32-35*

To put things in perspective, let's take this slowly. What Mary did here managed to provoke a heavenly response (in kind), the highest form of agreement you can think of. That agreement is expressed in the shortest verse in the Bible:

Jesus wept

He responded to Mary's weeping in agreement and the unthinkable happened. Her brother was raised to life again after four days in the grave.

Beloved, it doesn't matter whether the enemy had already scattered or shared out your body organs or consigned you to an evil coffin in the spirit, you can still deploy the tears of fire to provoke an aggressive response from heaven, right here, right now.

On a different note, many theologians have nicknamed Jeremiah the "weeping prophet." This is because prevailing opinion is that this prophet wept too much. But they have not stopped to study the prayers of the book of Jeremiah closely. And those who have even bothered tend to hastily conclude that God never answered his prayers. They miss the point.

The book of Jeremiah contains some of the most hard-boiled, aggressive prayers ever prayed. In fact, when I want to teach my inner circle students spiritual warfare, the book of Jeremiah is usually one of the top three upon which I focus. It is nothing short of a spiritual warfare manual for rainmakers all through the ages. Why else do you think that the prophet Daniel began his prophetic journey by studying this same book of Jeremiah?

That's food for thought.

Before we leave this section, let me quickly introduce you to our next rainmaker: King Hezekiah. Having just received a terrible death sentence from none other than the Lord, he remembered this one principle I'm sharing with you now.

Then things began to happen. This would lead us to one of the most powerful statements you will encounter in this manual.

Rainmaker #3: King Hezekiah Sheds Tears of Fire

Holy weeping is a secret weapon of healing and deliverance. It releases the tears of fire. It serves as a door opener into the realm of the miraculous. Of course King Hezekiah must have known this all along. So what did he do in the moment of crisis as he lay there, with the sentence of death hanging over his head?

> *Then Hezekiah turned his face toward the wall, and prayed unto the LORD,*
>
> *And said, "Remember now, O LORD, I beseech thee, how I have walked before thee in truth and with a perfect heart, and have done that which is good in thy sight." And Hezekiah wept sore.*
>
> *Isa 38:2-3*

Not only did this prayer warrior-king weep, he took things much further into another dimension. The Bible says he wept sore. Meaning he wept till he felt pains in his physical body. His chest must have been heaving. His lungs felt like exploding. He probably experienced what prophet Jeremiah meant when he wrote:

> *"Oh that my head were waters, and mine eyes a fountain of tears, that I might weep day and night . . ."*
>
> *Jer 9:1*

What happened after that? The Lord showed up and caused a reversal of the decree of death upon his life. I sometimes wonder how believers can accept satanic prophecies cloaked as medical advice from their doctors and other "well-meaning" advisors. Without bothering to consult the Alpha and Omega. In the case of Hezekiah, even when the message was delivered by the most prominent prophet of his time, he knew he could still raise a holy petition before the Lord.

I don't know about you, but I am with King Hezekiah here. As far as I'm concerned, only the Lord has the final say in the affairs of my life. And this leads us to:

Golden Statement 3:

Holy tears will always attract divine agreement and lift you into the level of anointing required to release your breakthroughs.

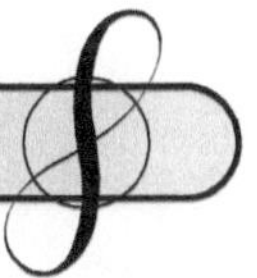

We can apply what we've learned so far. Here are the case studies we've just looked at:

1. Mary's tears at the tomb of Lazarus—Attracted the Lord's perfect agreement and opened the door to the miraculous.
2. Hezekiah's tears—Attracted the Lord's agreement through prophet Isaiah, leading to a reversal of a decree of death.
3. Hannah's tears—Brought agreement from Eli, the man of God. The Bible says it was the Lord who shut her womb. This same womb was unlocked as a result of the prayer of agreement.
4. The tears of Jesus Christ at Gethsemane—Attracted angels from heaven to strengthen Him so He could fulfill his divine assignment.
5. The cry of yours truly many years ago—Physically led me to contact a specific man of God to stand in agreement with me. The result? An entire satanic army was scattered and my breakthrough came on a platter of gold.

When the power of agreement is released in the heat of anointed prayer, so much that we consider impossible can become possible.

> *"Again I say unto you, that if two of you shall agree on earth as touching anything that they shall ask, it shall be done for them of my Father which is in heaven."*
>
> *Matt 18:19*

Please note that this type of divine partnership is always engineered from God's throne of grace. You can run up and down asking every Tom, Dick, and Harry to agree with you in prayer. It may not work. For agreement to yield true results, the Lord must be the matchmaker. For your part, you must be able to listen and discern His voice for the outpouring of rain to begin.

In summary, here are the 3 Golden Statements in this manual:

1. You must be prepared to confront every crisis at a level of anointing higher than the level that it took to create it.
2. "The Lord will never ignore the tears of His praying saints."
3. Holy tears will always attract divine agreement and lift you into the level of anointing required to release your breakthroughs.

Statement 1 confirms that you need to enter into a higher level of anointing today to break the yokes and undo the heavy burdens of many generations. But it would be an exercise

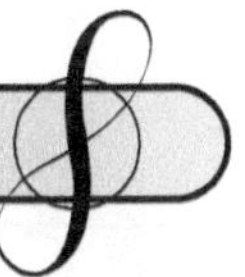

in self-delusion to think that modern day believers would be able to consistently operate in the realm of anointing that we've been describing, let alone to remain in that anointing for an extended period of time.

Here's the Good News. You can at least enter into this anointing from time to time, if you can bring holy tears before the Lord during prayer! Even those moments soaked in the anointing—no matter how fleeting—are enough to deal with many crises in your life because:

The LORD Will Never Ignore
The Tears of His Praying Saints!

We are getting ready to pray shortly. But first, there is one last thing that needs to be addressed before we move from theory to practice and apply what we've been studying in our PRAYERSHOCK sessions (coming up shortly).

Chapter Eight

When Others Are Engulfed in Flames

> *"The Spirit of the Lord is upon me, because he hath anointed me to preach the gospel to the poor; he hath sent me to heal the brokenhearted, to preach deliverance to the captives, and recovering of sight to the blind, to set at liberty them that are bruised, to preach the acceptable year of the Lord."*
>
> Luke 4:18-19

People may argue all they want about the principles shared in this book. But what they cannot argue about are the results, as you can see for yourself. Because at the end of the day, you must match up your results with what you see in the scriptures and then decide for yourself whether you are actually doing what Jesus called us to do.

> *Dear Elisha*
>
> *I thank you very much for all your help. I had serious problems in my marriage when i stumbled on your website. I really don't know how i got here but i found myself there. Anyway i want to give glory to GOD and thank you for your prayer points on how to turn a troubled relationship to terrific relationship. After barely three weeks of praying and fasting, my marriage was restored in ways i could have never imagined.*
>
> *I was headed for a divorce but knowing that it wasn't God's will for my marriage i trusted God to do things his way and lifted my marriage to him. It's really hard to believe sometimes when i look at my husband and think how he used to be and the words he used to say and giving me a guarantee that i should start living my life as a divorcee.*
>
> *Then i think oh our ways and our thoughts are not the same as GOD's. Indeed this God that we worship is true, faithful and alive and these prayer points, it's true that they have they been tested and proven to work. I thank you so much for all your help and may our good Lord continue to speak to you and give you wisdom to help others. God bless you.*
>
> *Sent by Pamela, United Kingdom on March 1, 2009*

As the saying goes, talk is cheap. Our Lord Jesus said as much to the Pharisees when they came against Him. And Brother Paul echoed the same sentiment when he wrote:

119

> *"For our gospel did not come to you in word only, <u>but also in power</u>, and in the Holy Spirit and in much assurance, as you know what kind of men we were among you for your sake."*
>
> *1 Thess. 1:5*

The gospel of Jesus Christ is more than just talk. Much more than talk! Anytime you begin to operate in the realm of the rainmakers, it is important to be humble and know that the Lord has called you into divine partnership with Him. He has enlisted you into His army to help rescue the dying, to pluck them right out of the fires of hell.

That's the reason Jesus Christ urgently wants to pour out His power upon those who are willing to receive the anointing for these end times. He does it so we can continue the work of His ministry here on earth:

> *"But ye shall receive power, after that the Holy Ghost is come upon you: and ye shall be witnesses unto me both in Jerusalem, and in all Judea, and in Samaria, and unto the uttermost part of the earth."*
>
> *Acts 1:8*

When you study this passage closely, you will see four specific groups of people where the anointing will lead us:

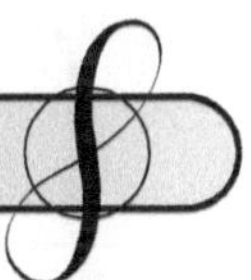

1. Jerusalem
2. Judea
3. Samaria
4. The uttermost parts of the earth

In other words, once we encounter the yoke-breaking, electrifying anointing of the Holy Ghost, we cannot keep it to ourselves. There are 4 specific groups of people in our world that the Lord wants us to reach for Him. We are to reach them with Christ's offer of salvation, healing and deliverance.

Some of us might feel drawn to one group more than the other. Here's what each group represents.

1. Jerusalem

Jerusalem refers to the group of people who are like you: friends, family, members of your community. You are to shine the light of the glorious gospel within your community without fear. As you do that, something inexplicable will begin to happen to you:

> *"And they that be wise shall shine as the brightness of the firmament; and they that turn many to righteousness as the stars forever and ever."*
>
> *Dan 12:3*

2. Judea

Judea represents our rulers; those in authority over us. What does the scripture say?

> *"I exhort therefore, that, first of all, supplications, prayers, intercessions, and giving of thanks, be made for all men;*
>
> *For kings, and for all that are in authority; that we may lead a quiet and peaceable life in all godliness and honesty.*
>
> *For this is good and acceptable in the sight of God our Savior;*
>
> *Who will have all men to be saved, and to come unto the knowledge of the truth."*
>
> 1 Tim 2:1-4

Note that this is a direct command from the Lord. It does not matter whether we like the rulers or whether we agree with their policies or not. The Word says to pray for them. Not to criticize them or make a career out of pointing out their every fault.

If you are reading this, here's a quick question for you: When last did you embark on a *fasting* and *prayer* program specifically to intercede for your leaders?

Maybe I should ask: when last did you become a mouthpiece to be used of the devil to criticize your leaders; or

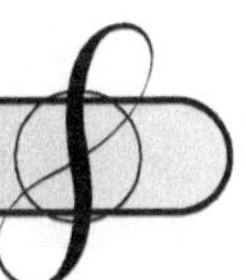

nod in agreement to someone criticizing them in the public square? Today? This week?

All I can say is please be careful. Why should you carry another person's evil load or partake in another man's sins? You may not know that many of the people on radio or television who speak evil about their leaders are pushing a hidden political agenda, even if they sometimes succeed in hiding it under the cloak of Christianity. But God knows the thoughts and the intent of men's hearts.

3. Samaria

Samaria represents people we do not like at all. Maybe they are not like us or they may look different from us. Or they offended us in the past. This is a tough one. Jesus says we must minister to them as well, after we've received the anointing for service.

> *"But I say unto you, Love your enemies, bless them that curse you, do good to them that hate you, and pray for them which despitefully use you, and persecute you;*
>
> *That ye may be the children of your Father which is in heaven: for he maketh his sun to rise on the evil and on the good, and sendeth rain on the just and on the unjust."*
>
> *Matt 5:44-45*

4. Uttermost Parts of the Earth

This last group refers to people in other corners of the earth. You can reach out to them by supporting missionaries with your finances and prayers. These are people who daily risk their lives for the sake of the gospel.

Our website, *www.firespringsministries.com*, is an end-of-the-earth ministry reaching thousands in 117 countries through the Internet. We are here to provide prayer resources for those who are similarly called to reach the ends of the earth for Christ. Clearly no one can do it without learning to pray effectively.

People appear from places we've never heard of before. The Lord brings them here to prepare them for the battles ahead. Many of our subscribers actually go on mission trips themselves, so they have a great opportunity to put into practice in the battlefront all they have been learning from this site. You may not be able to believe some of the exciting field reports coming in but here's the truth:

When you decide to step out of your boat of comfort for the Lord, He stands ready to back you up with signs and wonders anywhere He directs you to go for ministration. Here's one spectacular example from the West African nation of Senegal:

> *"Thank you for your teachings concerning dreams. After battling with a monster who was holding a young man captive in my dream. I was provoked to go to hospital to pray for HIV patients after a one week fasting and praying although I am not a pastor. In fact all the ten patients I prayed for tested negative, the doctors are now investigating on their medical records."*

This one was so amazing I asked for an update after 2 weeks. Here's the follow up email:

> *"Elisha, Thanks for your concern, As regards to my hospital invasion of two weeks ago I went back to the hospital on Tuesday to know whether the doctors had finished their investigations they started asking me some ignorant questions, like whether I have healed somebody with HIV before and what are the power behind my prayers.*
>
> *They turned me from one office to another and eventually told me to come after two days. Arriving there today I found out that they have discharged some of the patients who can now walk very well. The only patients left are the ones who had neither ate nor drank for so many months who are now learning to enjoy their food and drinks and sleep.*

> *The doctors refused to talk to me on the ground that my country is a country with over 95 percent muslims. Now I have decided to go to the streets to look for people with HIV and other incurable diseases and invite them for their healing . . ."*
>
> *Brother Innocent, Senegal*

Jesus said: "Behold, I send you forth as lambs among wolves . . ." Luke 10:3.

Here's another. This time the theater of action has shifted to Manila, Philippines.

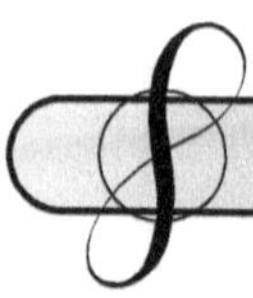

> *"I just came back from Manila Philippines in Asia.*
>
> *Thank you so much for your prayers. It was such a joy to know that I have people praying for me. Without prayer nothing happens. Thanks again for teaching me spiritual warfare prayers. I got an opportunity to use them in the Philippines. I give God all the glory. Spirits were manifesting and God was at work.*
>
> *The first night of the meeting there was so much repentance. The pastors cried out to God. It was such a blessing the way God moved.*

The Lord showed up unto his people. Many people were saved. It was such a blessing to see young people getting to know God. Four students were given new hearts. Two were scheduled for surgery. They went back to their doctors and the doctors were amazed.

Two people were given new kidneys. One was waiting for Kidney to be donated to her. The Lord created one for her. One woman had problem with her intestines, the Lord healed. The Lord healed so many who had kidney problems. The eyes were healed. Another woman had cancer the Lord healed her.

God moved in a way that even shocked me. A retired police officer had a stroke for four years the Lord healed him. He could not walk, but after prayer he started walking and he had feelings in his left arm which was paralysed.

God gave another soldier new bone marrow. One woman had water in her stomach, the doctors did try everything for her but nothing was helping her. She had spent all her savings. The Lord delivered her that night from witchcraft. The following day week she came and testified that the water that was causing her body to be swelling was gone. She looked like a pregnant woman. The Lord totally healed her.

One woman had epilepsy and goiter, as I started doing deliverance with her, the goitre left and the Lord delivered her. The other woman had tumor on her breast since 99, the Lord dissolved it. The other woman had problem with her lungs, after prayer she could breathe again.

127

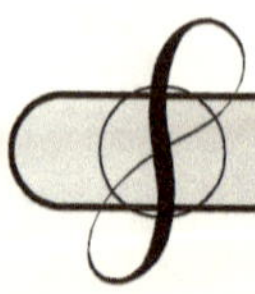

One young lady could not walk and she was bedridden for 6 months, she had a hole in her heart. The Lord healed. Sunday her mom came to church and she was just weeping. The Lord broke a lot of poverty in many people. The pastor and her husband——the Lord started restoring in their lives.

Marriages were restored. I had an opportunity to speak in the military camp. The Lord moved in the church. It was such a joy to see God at work. Last Friday one student was literally dying. She was in the hospital, the doctors told the parents to prepare for the funeral for their daughter. I prayed for her. Saturday the Lord moved and she was discharged. This was a miracle in itself. The whole family got saved.

The Lord showed up unto his people. Many people were saved. It was such a blessing to see young people getting to know God. The Lord performed so many miracles, healings and deliverances. I give God all the glory.

They are so many healings that took place. The pastor told me that the testimonies are still coming.

I give God all the glory. Thanks again for standing with me."

Sister Rita, Canada

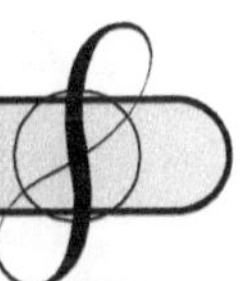

A Tale of Two Neighbors—Case Study

Finally here's an eye opening case study of how one of our Prayer Academy graduates stood in agreement with her neighbor to help recover a marriage that was on the brink of disaster.

> "*While praying step four prayers in* **Prayer Cookbook for Busy People**, *there is a prayer point where you say: 'I shall be an arrow in the hand of God to bring healing to His people.' God literally answered this one instantly. People have been waking me up early in the morning to tell me their problem—many of them marital problems—and I would quickly introduce them to Golden Key prayers.*
>
> *I applied Golden key prayers to my neighbor's situation—a wife thrown out by her husband. Last Sunday, August 19th, she showed up at my house at 6 AM, and confessed that she didn't know why she chose to come to me. I introduced her to the e-book, Point By Point and she said she would do anything to get her marriage back.*
>
> *She started the Esther fast on Tuesday and by Saturday her husband was looking for her everywhere. All through I prayed for her and asked Jehovah to intervene.* **Voila! The next Monday, she came to my office with a testimony.**

> *Her husband wants her back, no conditions. He has given her money and asked her to get a house to move in together!*
>
> **Elisha, it works!** *God is still in the business of blessing people.*"
>
> Sister Lilian, Kenya

One year later, the friend in this story sent me the following email confirmation:

> "*Am not new to your materials. My neighbor Lillian introduced me to your Prayer Guide for Busy People. My husband had thrown me out with the kids and never wanted anything to do with me again. I had given up from him and I never knew what to do anymore. One day I decided to give him the kids by abandoning them in the car. I couldn't sleep for two nights, so one day early in the morning I decided to go for them. I was met by a rude shock because my husband had not slept in the house which was full of his sisters who denied me access.*
>
> *As I stood at the closed door, my heart told me to knock at my neighbor's house. I really needed to talk to somebody. As she took me in she told me to stop fighting devils physically she asked me if I wanted my husband back. I told her that I would do anything apart from sin. So she gave me the prayer guide.*"

> *I did the Esther method and in the third day of the dry fasting my friend told me that my husband was looking for me and wanted to meet me to talk things over. I met him and he promised to take me back.*
>
> *I couldn't believe it since he was already seriously engaged to another lady and I was sure I had lost him. On the tenth day and the last day of fasting he came to me again. He gave me the house keys and a good amount of money to move to another house and my kids.*
>
> *His employer was taking him for training to the UK for two weeks. He came back after two weeks and promised to love me forever. He married me legally after some weeks and since then our life has never been the same.*
>
> *We have used the 101 prayer points to pray for a job and it came immediately after he lost the former one and anytime we want an instant answer to our prayers . . . your books have made my husband believe in God. Since then he is a changed man and I will always thank God for using you to reach people like me."*
>
> *Sister B., Kenya*

It didn't stop there. Here's a recent update concerning their situation:

> *"By the way Sister B., my friend whose husband had left and he came back to her very apologetic after 7 days of prayer and fasting using Point By Point, is doing very well. In fact, after that her husband started coming to church as a family, something that never used to happen. I have given her your contacts and the web addresses and have encouraged her to sign up for the newsletters and continue growing. Our God is an awesome GOD!!!"*
>
> *Sister Lilian, Kenya*

What did our Lord Jesus say?

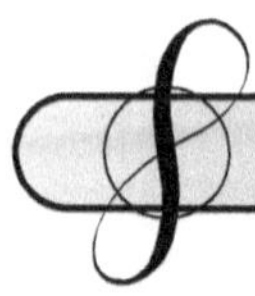

He said we should be our brother's keeper . . . or in this case, our sister's keeper.

If you've read this far, it may now be your turn to step out boldly for Jesus. Just look around you. There are endless situations crying out for divine intervention in your community. Are you willing to step up and stand in the gap?

The Lord wants you to be drenched in His power and anointing too. So you can become a powerful vessel to bring healing and deliverance to His people. He stands at the door and knocks. To hear Him you need to:

1. Surrender every department of your life to Jesus, leaving nothing out.

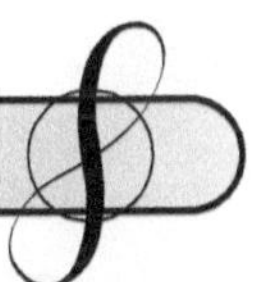

2. Repent from every known sin and turn away from them.
3. Become addicted to Bible study and prayer.
4. Become a true worshipper—one who worships the Lord in spirit and in truth.
5. Be divinely dissatisfied with your present level.
6. Develop a never-dying hunger and thirst for the anointing of the Holy Ghost.
7. Be an incurable giver—of your time, talent, resources to the service of God and to others around you.

Here's what the Lord is calling us to do:

> *Therefore He says:*
> *"Awake, you who sleep,*
> *Arise from the dead,*
> *And Christ will give you light."*
>
> Eph 5:14

If you are ready, let's now go to the prayers.

Chapter Nine

PRAYERSHOCK: Featuring The *Miracle Magnetizer* Prayer Sequences

Instructions:

If you miss one day of prayer, stay off and join the next batch.

Pray for all the members of the family.

Read 1 Corinthians 13 and act on it, live it every day.

This is a 21-day prayer sequence. You will pray the same prayer points nightly.

Here is my prayer for you before you begin:

> *"O Lord, by your grace, mercy, and love, you have helped me to nurture these ones this far. Even as you prayed for your disciples and us who were to join later in John chapter 15, Lord, I pray for these ones. I present them before you and I ask*

oh Lord, as we all wait upon you, pour out your Spirit upon us. Help us to live crucified lives. Help us to live victorious lives.

Lord Jesus, you chose Judas as one of your disciples, but he could not operate until you gave him the permission. And when the devil entered him, he could not stand your presence. Henceforth Lord, I pray for these ones that the devil will never be able to withstand these ones. I decree that they will not give the devil permission to operate in their lives.

For what concord has Christ with Belial? What agreement has he that believes with an infidel? Lord, I invite you into their lives. Be their God, work through them and in them. Break us and remold us, let your Spirit fall afresh upon us in Jesus Christ's name."

Amen.

Like a li'l acorn

that grows into a mighty tree

the prayers on the next page

will steadily grow into a mighty oak

of prosperity and divine health

if you will just take the time

to plant and nurture it

for 21 days straight.

The Prayershock Session

Begin with high praises; then read Isaiah 47, Nahum 3 out loud; and follow up with these prayers.

1. Every ancestral stronghold contending with my destiny, I pull you down in the name of Jesus.
2. Every evil king and queen mother claiming authority over my life, be dethroned; Jesus did not give you this authority, it shall not stand, be dethroned in Jesus' name.
3. Every ancestral soul tie operating in my life, break by the power in the mighty name of Jesus.
4. Special announcement: devil hear the Word of the Living God, whatever initiation anyone had entered into on my behalf that could give you a hold over my life, the blood of Jesus has separated me from every evil work. I am a new creature in Christ, old things have passed away; behold all things have become new in my life. It is written: the soul that sinneth, it shall die; a man shall bear his own judgment. You cannot hold me captive because of whatever relationship you had with my ancestors. I refuse to pay for what I know nothing about. What I do know is that Jesus Christ died and shed his blood for my atonement.

5. Every idol, evil king, evil queen mother, spiritual age group, strange children demanding sacrifice from my hands, receive the sacrifice of the blood of Jesus and lose your hold over my life in Jesus' name.
6. I release my soul from every evil cage by the power in the blood of Jesus. I cast down every evil imagination of household wickedness against my life in the name of Jesus.
7. Ministering angels of the Lord, search the land of the living, the dead, the dream world, satanic covens and bus stops and liberate my soul from captivity in the name of Jesus.
8. Ministering angels of the Lord, search the land of the living, the dead, the dream world, satanic covens and bus stops, and recover my stolen benefits, my glory, and my blessings in the name of Jesus.
9. You evil spiritual environment trying to control my physical life, receive the fire of the Lord and burn to ashes in the name of Jesus.
10. Every satanic timer set up against my life in the spirit, be scattered in the name of Jesus.
11. I bring the blood of Jesus against every evidence raised up by ancestral evil stronghold against my life and destiny in the name of Jesus.
12. I condemn every accusation raised up against me by the authorities of the dark kingdom by the blood of Jesus.

13. I silence every such accusation with the cross of Christ and the blood of Jesus.

14. Any person or personality using evil means to strengthen bondage in my life, bear your own judgment in the name of Jesus; for it is written: whatsoever a man sows that shall he reap.

15. I stand by the power of grace bestowed upon my life to choose and decree that no person, living or dead, can fashion the path of my life in Jesus' name.

16. O Lord my Father, arise in your anger and silence every satanic accusation against my destiny in the name of Jesus.

17. I command the wind, the ground, the sun, moon, and stars to work contrary to all evil authorities standing against my life in Jesus' name.

18. Any organ of my body that has been shared out in the spirit, I recover you now in the name of Jesus.

19. Let the blood of Jesus be transfused into my body now in the name of Jesus.

20. I wield the sword of the Lord and I cut to pieces any creature transforming itself into something else to attack me in the dream or in the physical. You evil creatures die now in the name of Jesus.

21. You stubborn pursuers of my life and family, turn back now and pursue your sponsors in the name of Jesus.

22. My life, receive power and authority to do exploits in Jesus' name.

23. Henceforth, I shall live every day of my life in the fear and knowledge of the Lord in Jesus' name.

24. O Lord, help me to be willing to serve others without expecting anything in return in Jesus' name.

25. I crucify my flesh at the cross of Christ. Henceforth Lord, not my will but let your will be done.

26. Holy Spirit, help me to love others unconditionally even as the Lord has commanded in Jesus, name.

27. (This is a 7-minute prayer) My life, receive fire in the name of Jesus.

28. (Take this one as a holy cry unto the Lord) Lord Jesus enter into my life and sup with me now.

29. (Read Psalm 24 in its entirety with a loud voice then make the following declaration) You the gate of my life open, and let the King of Glory come in and take His place in Jesus' name.

30. This is my time and season of manifestation. Thou power to mount up, fall upon me now in the mighty name of Jesus.

31. The voice of heaven over my life shall never be overpowered by the voice of the earth, for the earth is the Lord's in Jesus' name.

32. My life, receive the light of salvation and begin to shine in the name of Jesus.

33. My glory, arise and shine, for the glory of the Lord is risen upon you in Jesus' name.

34. Lord Jesus, I surrender my life to you; let your fire consume every evil seed in my life.

35. You intimidating spirits operating against my divine upliftment in life, be pulled down by fire in the mighty name of Jesus.
36. Every satanic plague programmed against my life from the moon, be roasted by fire in the name of Jesus.
37. Blood of Jesus, shield me and my family from satanic arrows fired from the sun, moon, and stars in Jesus' name.
38. O Light of God, illuminate every dark area of my life in Jesus' name.
39. Pentecostal fire of the upper room, fall upon me afresh as in the day of Pentecost in Jesus' name.
40. Every dormant talent in my life, come forth and explode for global recognition in the mighty name of Jesus.
41. I refuse to be detained by the powers of the grave in the name of Jesus.
42. Thou power of resurrection, fall upon every area of my life now in the name of Jesus (begin to name the areas one by one, such as marriage, finances, career, ministry, children, spouse, etc.)
43. I arise and move out of every evil environment by fire in the name of Jesus.

Thank the Lord for answering your prayers.

Chapter Ten

The Last Chapter:
An Email You Need to Read

How a Simple Question
Forced Me to Reveal a Deep Secret
About My Life.

> *"I need to ask about some possible prayer points, if they exist. If they do, I'm sure you would know about it.*
>
> *So then, are there any prayer points that can stop debt collection, repossession, or legal actions dead in their tracks?*
>
> *To be more specific, if one's car was being repossessed or one's home was being foreclosed on, what prayer points could be employed to stop these things dead in their tracks?*
>
> *Second, are there any points to bless or "multiply" one's sleeping hours?*
>
> *If one were always tired and fatigued, and normal sleep did not seem to bring proper energizing or refreshment, what prayer points would cover that?*

As of late, no matter how many hours sleep I get. I am always fatigued. I am really so weary and end up sleeping at work during breaks and lunch too.

I think when I start losing another hour at midnight, it is going to wipe me out.

I absolutely NEED to be able to stay awake at work, as I operate machinery.

Not to mention that sleeping on the job can result in getting fired!

If I start praying from, say, midnight to one, that will only leave me four hours sleep before I get up for work, so you see where this is leading?

I have to drive to work on four hours sleep then I have to operate machinery when I get there. This is not a good situation. I'm literally putting my life in jeopardy. (Not that it's worth a plugged nickel, anymore, anyway.)

It is going to be indispensable that I find a way for those four hour of sleep to be blessed, because for now I can't afford by any means to lose my job!

Man, I'm just simply worn out. Or as they say out in the country, I'm "plum tuckered."

The last time I prayed for 21 days and did the Esther fast, I started out like a sprinter but lost steam after awhile. The little engine thought he could, he thought he could, but he couldn't.

Perhaps you might emphasize to your people the importance of pacing themselves when they are going to go at it for 21 days straight. Three weeks is a long time to go at it hard and fast, and some of us were not made for that kind of grueling pace, me thinks.

Some folks are great sprinters, but God didn't make everyone a marathon runner.

Isn't it better to keep going moderately but steadily, rather than taking off like a jack rabbit from day one and running out of steam before it's all over?

(The old tortoise and the hare.)

Anyway, I killed myself during the last one, and I have never quite recovered. At fifty two, I'm not quite physically as able as I once was.

My metabolism seems to be slowing down a bit. It doesn't help, either, that I am not hardly eating. I wonder how many others there are out there like me?

Well, to conclude, and wrap up, I am hoping you can tell me some prayer points for stopping creditors and repossession efforts dead in their tracks, and for multiplying the effects of one's sleep.

I have forgiven those who have hurt me . . . Amen"

Reader from Indiana, USA

If You Are Looking for Sympathy,
My Response Might Shock the Daylights Out of You!

My Response:

Dear D.,

Thank you for sharing your heart in all these emails.

I can quite remember in the early 1990s I was all but wiped out too. Thankfully no lives were lost but there were close calls a few times.

At the time, I lost everything; didn't even have a roof over my head. My spouse and I, we had to wander around until a wonderful Christian brother allowed us to stay in his living room.

I had become so fed up with the rosy prophecies I received for many years. Meanwhile things got worse and worse. Then one day, in His supreme wisdom the Lord led me to a church where they spent 70% of the time praying.

The only trouble was that I couldn't afford the bus fare to get to church and back. I'm talking 15 miles round trip. By this time the Lord had rekindled a fire in my spirit. And I made a decision to walk to church, 3 times a week (Sunday, Monday, Wednesday) so I could participate in those earth-shaking prayers.

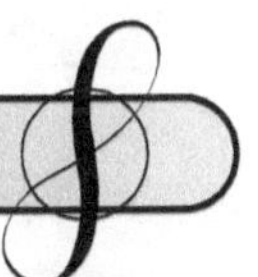

I remember walking back from a hot Wednesday night prayer meeting. There was no food in the house as usual. It would take me till midnight to walk back to where I called home.

I was tired and thirsty and I couldn't even afford a bottle of spring water on the way. But there was joy inside my spirit that I could not explain.

Then suddenly the Lord spoke to me very clearly.

And here's what He said:

"Son, you are in the training school of the Holy Spirit. How long you remain in this situation is totally up to you. As soon as you learn the lessons you will be promoted to the next level.

If you refuse to learn now, you will continue to stay in this wilderness. Because where I'm taking you requires the kind of tough military training you are going through just now.

So far, you are doing well."

The message ended as abruptly as it had started. But right from that moment my entire life was transformed. I was now able to embrace the kind of affliction I was going through without murmuring or complaining.

I knew in my spirit that it was just a matter of time.

Now, my situation didn't change or disappear overnight. It dragged on and on but I was getting dangerously toughened in the spirit. By the time the turnaround happened I'd advanced to the point that nothing else mattered.

Looking back now, that was probably one of the most blessed periods of my life. The deep insights into prayer I now share were learned under those trying circumstances.

Yes, all the prayer points and strategies I teach now, were perfected in those days, in the furnace of affliction. We are now heading into the 21-day program. You may find prayer points here and there that look alike but I doubt that you will ever find them in the sequence that I share.

The Lord made me to understand the mystery of prayer sequences in those days. And years ago when I was walking the streets of Michigan, I had ample opportunity to fine-tune them.

Now I just gave you a bit about myself so you understand that there is a price to pay for spiritual power and authority. Not quite as easy as TV preachers make everything sound. Now back to your situation. When we prayed for you last night, the Lord told us you had to start on a clean slate. You may know what that means.

I recently asked one of my eagle-eyed prayer warriors to pray for you. She told me point-blank that you needed to do some foundational work FIRST. I believe she sent you an email explaining certain things. You need to take that email seriously.

On the prayer points you requested, none of them will work until you have cleared your foundation thoroughly. Given your situation, you DON'T need to fast. You don't need to do your praying at the midnight hour either. Rather, what I would ask you to do is convert your lunch break into prayer time.

I have personally done this before in the past, so it is not theory I'm telling you. Every advice I dispense from my website, I have personally used it in the past, when everything was upside down for me.

Until the Lord righted the ship of my destiny and saved me from sinking.

I am called a prayer warrior. My language and ministry is tough. But if you can follow through on what I tell you, the ONE who sent me will prove Himself to you.

Now, it is time to get ready for a massive assault. The devil is a warmonger. The only language he understands is violence. And boy, is he going to see war in the next 21 days! I make no pretence as to what I bring to the table. It is sink or swim, do or die interruption prayers that work in the real world.

I caution people who want to order my materials not to bother if they are not going to stay the course. Or if they are easily offended. Why? Because the way I receive the message is the way I deliver it. No softening or "sugar-coating" of the message here.

At the end of the day, the ONE who sent me is standing behind all this to confirm it. And that's why I can confidently say that testimonies and praise reports will start coming in from day one.

What are you going to see in the next 21 days? It doesn't come in a box, and it doesn't melt in your mouth. It's not glittery and shiny; it doesn't cost an arm and a leg. It's easy to unwrap, and it's easy to fall in love with the results.

I am pumped up right now. I'm ready to explode; my fingers are on the trigger. I know that many will start this and not be able to follow through, and we'll do our best to pray for them.

But the march must continue. And I pray you will diligently consider all I have said. It is time to pray. Let's quit talking and do our part. And watch the Lord do His own part.

God bless you!

elisha

After Only 21 Days in the Prayer Cockpit (*Prayer Academy*), Our Intrepid Prayer Warrior Now Sings a Different Tune!

Elisha,

Well, it is almost over, but I couldn't wait to say this: In all my life, I never dreamed such powerful dynamite prayers even existed!

These prayer points have been incredible beyond words! Surely, they are the best in the world. The old saying, "Give a man a fish and you feed him for a day. Teach him to fish and you feed him for a lifetime," certainly applies here!

With these prayer points under my belt, I feel as if I have been equipped to pray (or fish) for an entire lifetime. They are so 200% thorough, and you have left nothing to chance, nor have you left anything out. With these points, you have come at the devil from the front, back, top, bottom, and every other possible conceivable angle! He is literally left with no place to hide, no breathing room, and no mercy. Just the way I like it!

149

I will say this: I never in my life dreamed I had so many
ranks and types of enemies! Enemies in the waters, en
the air, demons, wasters, spiritual vampires, satanic
strongmen, witches, marine spirits, snakes, scorpions,
that mess with the moon and stars, generational spiri
tive parental spirits, spirits of anger, Ahab, criticisms
jezebel, infirmity, pride, hatred, worry, selfishness, impa
fear, wrong speaking, competition, adultery, prayer
lukewarmness, failure, cruelty, abuse, unfaithfulnes
sliding, discouragement, scarcity, and on and on the
goes!!!

Whew!!! It's enough to make your head spin!

What a motley, scummy bunch the devil has organizec
the Lord of hosts and his Christ!! It's incredible to th
most Christians have no inkling of the hoards they
against, let alone how to pray against them!

When you think about it, with all the demonic hoard
up against anyone wanting to live for Christ, it's onl
miracle of God's grace that anyone makes it safely th
heaven!

Most Christians just go about in their happy bliss, ha
idea of the sinister, dark hordes of demonic ilk that w

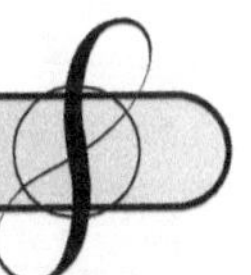

absolutely obliterate them and their testimony. If they could glimpse into the spiritual realm for a brief second, they would probably pass out from utter shock!

Anyway, I have to go now. Again, thank you for sharing these Incredible, explosive dynamite, prayer points/weapons with us! I feel equipped for a lifetime! From the Holy Spirit, during this Prayer Academy, I have learned this: these prayer points are just a beginning. A beginning of a new and different lifestyle!

Once the devil is flushed out, like a cancer, one has to be diligent every day and continue to take an aggressive, warlike stance and make continued advances into enemy territory, because to stand still is to lose ground.

No? Like a cancer that has gone into remission, continued lifetime diligence and aggression is required to prevent the cancer from returning with a vengeance. Except in this case, the "cancer" happens to be the devil and his cronies.

Gotta run,
From Indiana, USA

RESTRICTED READING
An Example Prayer Coaching Session

Why Catherine Is No Longer in Tears

Dear Friend,

If you had seen Catherine that day, you'd know why she needed a miracle. Her best friend had just tested positive for a cancerous tumor on her breast. Things became so bad, she was rushed to the hospital and started on a chemotherapy regime. She even had to be forced to eat by her doctors.

Catherine first began to react in a natural manner, crying and asking why, oh why, with limited success. But then it occurred to her there might be a spiritual side to this. That's when she switched to prayer and requested a coaching session with battle tested "prayer bullets" from the Prayer Academy.

An amazing thing happened: after faithfully applying the prayer prescription every day for seven days, her friend's cancer disappeared without a trace! She feels fine! So fine she's back celebrating the victory with friends and family. The entire ordeal lasted two months.

152

The following email sequence tells her story:

Email 1: Catherine's Sad Story
April 3, 2007

> *Dear Elisha,*
>
> *Please allow me to tell you something . . . I am in tears as I write you this email, my best friend has been tested for a cancerous tumor on her breast and it has come out positive, regardless of what all the doctors say I have asked her to join me as we do a 3-day dry fast and ask for the healing from God. I am so positive about it. Could you also send me prayer points on that? Currently am using my old emails from you for prayers. Please Elisha, remember us in this as you pray also.*
>
> *May God bless you,*
> *Catherine, Kenya*

Email 2: My Response
April 3, 2007

> *Dear Catherine,*
>
> *Use the prayer points in the "Prayer of Caleb" book. Do the 3-day Esther fast. Add 4 days of partial fasting. Bringing it to 7 days.*

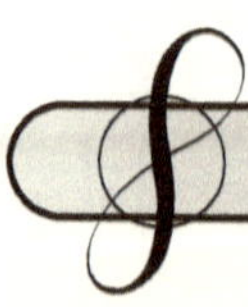

On the 7th day, the 2 of you should break bread together (i.e., take communion), then prepare and send a memorial offering to any ministry of your choice (it could even be an orphanage), and make it a point to wake up at midnight to PRAISE the Lord from time to time. Then when the Holy Spirit prompts you, tell your friend to go back for the test.

The Lord will give you an answer of peace!

elisha

Email 3: Catherine's Testimony
June 15, 2007

Dear Elisha,

My name is Catherine and I am in Kenya. You remember me writing you a mail in a desperate situation when my best friend was discovered to have breast cancer?

Well as I wrote that mail I was in tears, here again writing to you still in tears; tears of joy!

We did as you advised and before the first day of the Esther fast was over, she was put in the hospital and that night they started her on a chemotherapy dose, so I continued with the fast as she was forced to eat by the doctors. We did the midnight prayers at the same time of the night though from different places (she was using the Prayer of Caleb book as you

had advised). She has gone through 3 chemo doses and on 4th June they took her in for surgery and removed the lump from her breast, they took it to the laboratory and it has not shown any results of cancer or even its traces!! They are yet to give an explanation to this. Other laboratories have been given the sample of the lump to test and so far nothing shows cancer cells, please note that her initial slide has been re-tested and it proves that she actually had cancer of the breast. Now this is being discussed amongst the doctors as they wonder what could have happened, even the victim is still saying she thinks it is a dream, but of course this is the reality. (The news was broken yesterday and I will keep you posted).

What men cannot do God has a solution. Do you have any set of thanksgiving prayers? My strength in prayer and faith in God has been added by this miracle in a way I can't explain.

Yours in Christ,
Catherine

Email 4: Catherine's Update
June 24, 2007

Dear Elisha,

I hope you are well, just a quick update as I promised to keep you posted. It has really been confirmed through writing that my best friend is cancer free!!! We are still in celebration, I don't think we will be able to overcome the excitement.

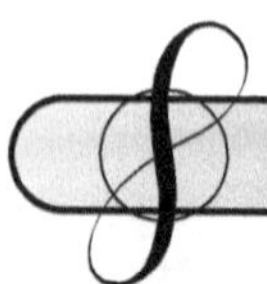

> *She has told me that on Wednesday she had a strong feeling from deep within her that she should go to one orphanage and get a kid to be taking care of; (in terms of clothes and upkeep while the kid remain in the orphanage) she has said that she feels doing something like this for the Lord who has got her from the valley of death, would be showing appreciation.*
>
> *She says that she wakes up in the night to give thanks to God but can't stop crying, marveling at the greatness of the Lord.*
>
> *I am waiting for the set of prayers I requested from you and I must confess to you that even I didn't expect results that fast! 2 months!!!*
>
> *Thanks for using my testimony to encourage others that our Lord still answers prayers.*
>
> *Yours in Christ,*
> *Catherine*

This all happened in 2007. End of story, Right? Wrong! Wait until you hear what happened next . . .

Over one year later, on a cold, snowy December morning, I opened my inbox to find this:

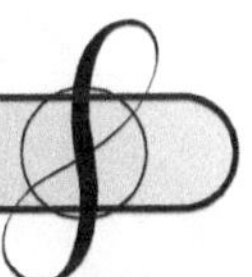

Catherine's Friend Shows Up and Confirms Report
December 28, 2008!

Morning Elisha,

I am Catherine's Friend!

I am writing to you this mail at 12.01 am.

My name is Christine, and believe it or not, I am Catherine's best friend, Catherine from Kenya, the one in your testimony of her friend who was diagnosed with breast cancer but is now healed.

That is me.

Elisha, I don't know what to write to you but I have this strong feeling to talk to you.

Here's my story . . .

I was diagnosed with a tumor in my breast on April 3rd last year as Catherine told you. i had no idea she was seeking prayer assistance from you, until a few months ago I logged into your website and found her testimony.

> *At that moment, I was looking for a car on the Internet but it had seemed impossible to get one and I was losing my faith. Then God led me to your website!*
>
> *Elisha every time I read this testimony I cry uncontrollably as I am now, because of God's immeasurable love for undeserving me. I thank him every day for this miracle.*
>
> *I have since subscribed to your newsletters and would like to kindly ask you to send me thanksgiving prayer points.*
>
> *There is more, the Lord did not only heal me from the cancer but he also gave me a new car and a new job! I have been using some of the prayer points from your newsletter.*
>
> *May the good Lord bless you and your family.*
>
> *Christine, Kenya*

Thank God for Christine and her dear friend Catherine. This is just one example of a prayer coaching session and the results.

Now back to you. Would you like to discover how to become so good at praying effective prayers that you never again need to wonder whether God really answers prayers?

Other Books in the Series

Book One

Prayer Cookbook for Busy People

*T*here is a method to pray and receive the most desirable blessings promised in the Bible. It is called:

The Esther Method

Those who apply the Esther Method as explained in this book have received blessings, such as:

> *"I received a check of over $1000 in the mail, new car, brand new home, plus a new position with a Fortune 100 company . . . all within 2 months of using these principles (Note: 2 banks recently advised me to file for bankruptcy because of my credit!).*
>
> *I've never experienced this kind of rapid breakthroughs in all my years as a Christian and intercessor"*
>
> Rebecca A., Washington

The Esther method even helps you to receive divine supply from God's own storehouse.

> *"My husband and I were involved in the 21-day prayer marathon. Within 3 weeks, we had our first major breakthrough! We had a very unexpected resource send a check in the amount of $5,000! This is the exact amount I had prayed for. We give God the glory!! Thank you so very much for teaching others the 'scriptural way' of prayer. God bless you continually."*
>
> *Cindy H., Ohio*

The Esther Method helps you realize the enormous potential you have as a child of God.

> *"I am so elated!!! Remember my 'frustrated first lady' letter I sent you? Your response to me was entitled 'empowered first lady.' You told me to use my problems as an opportunity that God can use to teach 'your hands to war and your fingers to fight.'*
>
> *Well Elisha, the prayer marathon taught me just how to do that. The Lord opened up my understanding so much and gave me victory! I cannot believe that in such a short time since I started the marathon, within the second week I was having victories even with my marriage. Right now my husband is the sweetest thing, it's like we just got married!!!"*
>
> *Newly Empowered Lady, Ontario*

The Most Effective Prayer Method Ever!

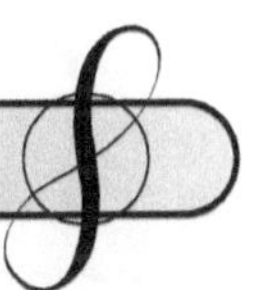

Can I ask you something? Would you like to have the ability to:

○ Pray and receive an answer from the throne of grace and watch joyfully as it manifests physically for you to enjoy?

○ Wake up every morning, excited about your day, knowing the Lord has truly loaded that day with benefits just for you, just as He promised?

○ Have complete strangers walk up to you and give you precisely the things you prayed for that morning?

○ Receive turnaround breakthroughs in your career, your business, as well as in your relationships?

○ Pray the type of prayers to heal your body and mind, especially your emotions?

○ Know how to pray and demolish loneliness, depression, and frustration out of your life?

○ Know how to slam the door shut against financial embarrassment?

○ Be the trusted ONE people can turn to for help when they need spiritual direction?

This book changes the way you see prayer and empowers you to take advantage of this God-given but long-neglected gift. In this handbook you will find a breakdown, chapter-by-chapter, of this prayer principle that has helped hundreds of Christians just like you to finally realize their dreams in every area of their lives.

Within the handbook you'll find how three simple steps can help you see the power of the Esther Method. You'll also find these topics (to list but a few):

- Prayer Attraction
- The 7 Deadly Prayer Killers
- Spiritual Timing
- Signals of Answered Prayer
- Secrets of Prayer Points
- Prayer Triggers
- Mystery of Silence
- Positioning
- How To *Never* Be Anxious Again
- Speed Prayer
- Unclaimed Blessings
- The 60-Minute Timeline
- Mystery of Isaiah 58
- Golden Key Secret
- The Back-Door Principle
- Spaceship Analogy
- The 3-Day Rule

And much more.

There is a "back door" in heaven. This door is highly confidential. It is reserved for a small group of men and women who need to get answers to their prayers very quickly. (Note: you may choose to belong to this elite group anytime you wish). It

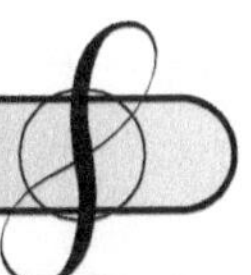

> *provides a shortcut into the storehouse of God. Maybe you've noticed that when certain people pray, the answers come very quickly, whereas for some other people, the answer takes forever to come . . . if it comes at all!*
>
> *What's the difference? The former group knows how to access the back door to heaven while the latter is ignorant of its existence. And what a great difference this makes.*
>
>

Part 2, "Heaven Has A Back Door," page 20
Prayer Cookbook for Busy People

> *"Remember the block of land I told you we've been trying to sell for months without success? After my Esther Fast on Monday, the bank rang my husband on Tuesday with an offer from this one buyer... and we just made a tidy profit of $50,459.75!"*
>
>

Sisilia H., Australia

What Is the Esther Method, Anyway?

The Esther Method is a practical, Bible-based method that allows *any* Christian from any denominational background to receive the desired answers to their prayers, sometimes in as short a period as 10 days.

Prayer Cookbook for Busy People teaches The Esther Method as a step-by-step system.

The method is in the Bible. This handbook is like a spiritual roadmap to show you and help you manifest the promises of God for your life *as fast as possible*, but you must be willing to invest the time to read the book and pray the prayers. If you will make up your mind to do just that, every step from now on will be a step in the right direction.

"I have great news to share with you. I took in the prayer marathon December and prayed for my finances, the ministry that God has for me and my future spouse. January the 17th my husband to be came into my life and we are going to be married in June, is that not WONDERFUL!!!, I am so happy. God is GOOD."

Maggie L., South Africa

"Yes! And to the glory of GOD, I am able to testify that I just landed my dream job with an oil and gas company!!!! This is the fruit of the Prayerthon we did up until Christmas. I cannot believe the package. It is more than 100% above what I currently earn!"

Bola E., Lagos, Nigeria

"Your prayer points are 'spiritual hand grenades' and 'spiritual nuclear warheads' demolishing the seen and the unseen! Praise God."

Johnny O., Australia

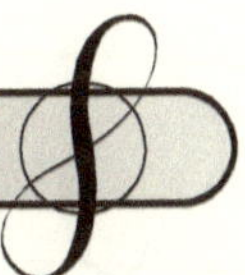

> *"The teachings and prayers since my introduction to your ministry back in October or so have been the most productive and enlightening phase of my Christian journey."*
>
> *Pastor Eunice, Washington, DC*

Now to the Questions

I Don't Want to Wait Till Eternity to Receive Answers to My Prayers. Will These Principles Work Fast Enough?

This is one of the most common questions people ask me. I want you to know that miracles, breakthroughs, almost any kind of blessing you can imagine, will have an uncontrollable attraction toward you. You may not be able to see this if your spiritual eyes are not yet open. You will feel the satisfaction of seeing some of the things you had longed for and prayed about without success suddenly tossed in your lap when you dig into these prayers in earnest.

Do I Need Be a Pastor, Minister, or Believer of Many Years Standing for These Principles to Work?

Absolutely not! These principles work for any Christian, who is living according to biblical standards. It doesn't matter if you've been a Christian for 20 years or you just gave your life to the Lord Jesus two weeks ago. In fact, in reality, sometimes a young believer (without a lot of confusing teachings in her head) does end up getting better and faster answers!

Spiritual or Material Blessings—Your Choice!

Everyone wants something different in life. *Prayer Cookbook for Busy People* teaches you how to receive blessings through prayer, in the most effective way possible. By using these biblical secrets and step-by-step outlines, you can transform your life and relationships into something close to heaven on earth. The Esther Method works whether you desire a closer spiritual walk with the Lord or you want His promises of abundance, peace, and joy to flood your life.

I invite you to come on board with thousands of other believers who are having dramatic success in their lives and relationships, and download *Prayer Cookbook for Busy People* here right now.

http://www.prayercookbook.com

OTHER BOOKS IN THE SERIES

BOOK TWO

Point By Point:
101 Prayers for Marriages

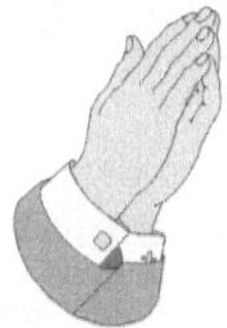

You Are About to Learn How to Stop Divorce Proceedings and Save Your Marriage

From Frustration To Restoration
In 14 Short Days!!

"I am so elated!!! Remember my 'frustrated first lady' letter I sent you? Your response to me was entitled 'empowered first lady'. You told me to use my problems as an opportunity that God can use to teach 'your hands to war and your fingers to fight.'

Well Elisha, the prayer marathon taught me just how to do that. The Lord open up my understanding so much and gave me victory! I cannot believe that in such a short time since I started the marathon, within the second week I was having victories even with my marriage. Right now my husband is the sweetest thing, it's like we just got married!!!"

Newly Empowered Lady, Ontario

Dear Christian Friend,

Let me ask you three questions. How would you like to know the ONE biblical principle that can save your marriage or relationship right now? How would you like to know how to guarantee peace of mind in your marriage? How would you like to learn the secret of keeping your marriage going strong, year after year?

If at this very moment you are feeling desperate, frustrated, alone, or even scared (or maybe just plain mad) when it comes to your marriage, that probably sounds almost too far-fetched to be true, right? But what if the answers, as you will see in a few seconds, are absolutely Yes!

172

Dear Elisha,

It's been pretty tough. When I stopped praying those prayer points that you emailed me. I slacked in fasting, praying and reading God's word. I had to repent ask GOD for forgiveness and start all over. Look as though everything went wrong.

Before, I got in my comfort zone of not fasting and praying nor reading God's word. I prayed some of those prayer points, God brought me and my ex-husband back together after twenty-three years of divorce.

> *We got into an argument. I'm not speaking to him and he's not speaking to me right now. The Lord brought to my attention to fast all this week, fight for what's mine, take back what the devil has stolen by fasting and praying and by using the prayer points, and to ask my ex-husband for forgiveness as well as he should do the same for me.*
>
> *GOD says not just to pray for me and my ex-husband but for other married couples who having marital problems as well. I praised the Lord for you and your beautiful work in the ministry."*
>
> *Joanne R., Seattle*

Let me explain by quickly telling you a true life story. On a beautiful spring morning 25 years ago, two young women wedded at the same church. The two women were very much alike. Both had been brought up by Christian parents, both were beautiful, and both were filled with wonderful dreams about the future (as young women are).

Recently, these women returned to the church for their 25th wedding anniversary. They were still very much alike. Both were still married. Both had three children. And both, it turned out, had husbands who worked for the same technology company in different states.

But there *was* a difference. One of the women has been struggling in her marriage for years and it showed. She

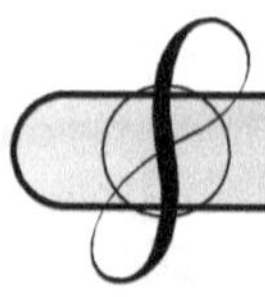

looked drawn and tired. She had been close to divorce three times in the past. Just two weeks before this event, she'd made a shocking discovery. Her husband was having a secret affair in the office!

And the other woman? Her family was the closest thing to heavenly bliss and it showed. There was a sparkle in her eyes and a spring to her steps as she walked around hand in hand with her husband. What made the difference?

Have you ever wondered, as I have, what makes these kinds of difference in people's marriages? It isn't always dedication or talent or beauty. It isn't that one person wants her marriage to succeed and the other doesn't.

174

"He Came Back To Me—Suddenly! I must say I have been truly blessed! I was going through a rough time in my relationship and I had decided to give up . . . I prayed and asked the Lord to work with us through this. I even thought God wanted us apart.

I then had my mind set on giving up when he (suddenly) came back and now we are seriously working on a bright future together!

Thank you for your help and guidance through the Prayer Marathon."

Sis. Ann, New York

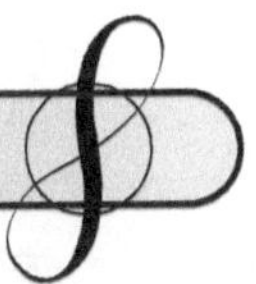

The difference lies in what each person knows about spiritual things and how he or she makes use of that knowledge.

And that is why I am writing to you about a new prayer manual, *Point By Point: The 101 Prayers that Strengthen Marriages and Relationships*. For that is the whole purpose of the book: To give its readers spiritual knowledge—and how to apply that knowledge in prayer.

A Prayer Book on Marriages and Relationships Unlike Any Other

You see, *Point By Point* is a unique prayer manual. It contains little-known spiritual insights about marriage that you won't find in any other book. It includes 101 prayer points that address every area of marriage that you can think of, be it finances, health, or faithfulness to the marital vows.

Here's a Deep Secret For You . . .

There is a prayer point for every conceivable situation in your marriage. Right now I am looking at the prayer points for day one. It contains relevant scriptures and powerful confessions.

Every spiritual scenario that can possibly affect your marriage in the physical is covered; from lack of finances, unfaithfulness, marriage curses, inherited patterns from the mother's and father's bloodlines, to ungodly influences and competition from strange men or women.

And there is page after page inside this prayer manual, filled with nuggets of rare spiritual information that's useful to *you*. A daily supply of relationship-building scriptures helps keep you spiritually alert and sensitive.

Confessions to activate the presence of God over your marriage is laid out, word for word, together with the times to use them for maximum effect. In this revised edition, the prayer points have been honed, refined and polished into something that resembles a step-by-step recipe that anyone can follow as easy as baking a cake.

There are never-before-revealed prayer secrets you can use to turn troubled relationships to terrific relationships in as little as 14 days. One sister told me, "My marriage experienced a turnaround . . . there is love, joy, and peace in my home where before there was chaos."

These prayer points will help:

- Saturate your relationship with love that keeps your spouse sticking to you like glue.
- Make your marriage impossible to break.
- Close any spiritual loophole in your spouse's heart and mind with the blood of Jesus.
- Add love, happiness, and joy to your relationships.

No matter how you look.

Or how old you are.

Or how much you weigh.

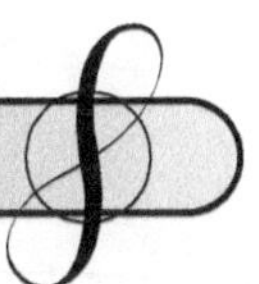

Those who learn these prayers have a definite advantage over those who don't.

Here's what this type of prayer does:

- It saturates your relationship with enduring love and affection.
- It generates the full support of both family and friends.
- It clears conflicts created by nosy and manipulative in-laws.
- It totally eliminates plans for separation and divorce.
- It restores love that you can almost feel and touch.
- It dramatically increases your spouse's desire to remain faithful to the marital vows.
- It maintains a warm and friendly atmosphere in the home.
- It acts as an impenetrable "firewall" against unwanted attention from "strange" men and women.

Everything is spelled out for you. Nothing is left to chance or guesswork: the time to pray, what to say, what to expect, it's all here. This kind of prayer has been used for centuries by the most successful and the most highly-desired Christian couples. And now, you too can use it, if you:

- Need to strengthen your marriage
- Are struggling too hard in your marriage
- Worried about how long your marriage will last

You will find that these godly prayers work, even if:

You've ever experienced conflict and hostility in the home, you get the prayers to sweeten these relationships.

Note: these are completely ignored secrets in the Bible that only a few people bother to learn. *(After praying these prayer points, one woman remarked that if she had this book in her hand just last year, her marriage will still be intact by now).*

Your life starts to change as soon as you get this material in your hands.

- Because you'll learn how the women of old were taught, and the prayers they used, to keep their marriages together.
  (**Hint:** after they learned this secret, separation or divorce became a thing of the past).
- Because you'll learn how to pray spicy prayers that would make your spouse enthusiastically want to stay married to you forever.
- (No games or manipulation here; it's been in the Bible all the time).
- Because you'll discover the two deadly signals that could bring marriages to a screeching halt and learn how to avoid them.
- Because you'll learn to pray scripture-based prayer points that break every spell and hypnotic suggestion off your spouse—and off you for that matter. (Please don't laugh; home breakers use spells all the time)!

O Because you'll discover little-known prayer points
that literally dissolve plans for separation and divorce.

And much, much more.

You may just be one prayer away from a tide-turning
breakthrough in your marriage. This is the most biblical
(and easiest) way to strengthen your marriage or any other
relationship you'll ever come across. Plus, this is seriously
important information for you in the times in which we
live; a time when the divorce rate among Christians and
non-Christians alike has gone through the roof!

Now you too can discover the principles that one of the
two women I described in the beginning of this letter has
been using to keep her marriage going strong for 25 years,
while for the other woman, divorce is staring her right in the
face.

No matter what the marriage psychologists tell you, the
security of your marriage will always rest on your relationship
with Jesus and the kind of prayers you pray! All the pop
psychology and the feel-good material you see on television
and the Internet can *never* solve any spiritual problems.

About those 2 women I mentioned earlier. They were
wedded on the same day, in the same church, by the same
pastor. The same marital blessings were pronounced on
both. So what made their marriages so different?

179

Spiritual knowledge, converted to prayer points and applied without hesitation—an investment in success. I cannot promise you that marital success will be instantly yours if you start using *Point By Point,* but I can guarantee you will find that your marriage—indeed your entire life—will begin to take a turn for the better and those dreams you had on your wedding day (now long dead) will slowly but surely begin to come alive as you apply these simple principles consistently.

For more details on how to order, please go to the following link:

http://www.unlockmymarriage.com

Other Books in the Series

Book Three

Prayer DNA Secrets

Have you been told that you can create your own miracles? But when you try to get advice on how to actually do it, you find that no one can quite tell you how?

The Scripture Has a Lot to Say About This

Take my case for example. Just like most people, I started out praying and receiving zero answers for my efforts. But one day the Lord had mercy on me and showed me how to claim the promises in the Bible in my life through prayer. Then He showed me how to manifest those promises even faster by adding a peculiar kind of fasting to my prayers. I like to joke that I stumbled on an "ancient" secret in the Old

Testament but the reality is that He led me to it at His appointed time.

The result: I got a dream job that paid five times more than I earned previously; the joy of my marriage was restored; I received a new house and a new car the same day, and I started a thriving home business. Not long after, this online ministry followed.

I've Also Helped 3,187 Other Christians Online to Do the Same Thing

This includes a sister in Australia, and another in Texas. All of them are wonderful Christian folks just like you, and all of them received multiple blessings that God promised in the Bible within a month of following the simple advice I was led to share with them.

"From Zero to $50,459.75 Profit
in Less Than 30 Days"

Hello Elisha,

I just want to update you on what our Awesome God through your guided prayers is doing in our lives.

Remember my last email on Monday 12th September, I said that I felt God will do a speedy miracle for me this week because I did the Esther 3 days/night fast again.

Guess what brother!! Remember the block of land that I said that we made a profit of $40,000.00? Well for your information the bank rang my husband on Tuesday, and said that we have actually made a profit of $50,459.75!!

Praise the Lord, the Glory is his alone. The money will be in the bank on Wednesday next week. I stand in awe of this God. I believe so much in this specific power point prayers, it works brother. It gives me confidence to keep going.

I print everything that you send me and keep them in a folder for reference. I enjoy reading and experimenting with those prayer points, it is so powerful.

I DEFY ANYBODY THAT SAYS THIS PRAYER DOES NOT WORK!!

I am smiling everyday and so is my family. I give our Heavenly Father all the Glory.

Sister Sisi, Australia

*"Harvest of Miracles Money, New Car and
Now a Home of My Own . . . All Within 2 Months!"*

Elisha,

This principle you taught works indeed. I've never experienced this kind of breakthrough with all my years as a Christian and intercessor.

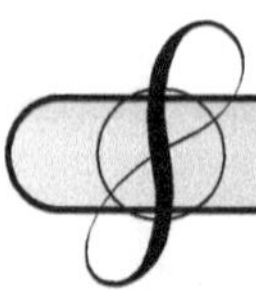

I received over one thousand dollar check in the mail about a case that was filed against my employer, class action suit.

Another miracle about a house.

You know I was supposed to leave the place I'm residing now by the end of this month, October. Well, I was so sure in my spirit that God would make a way for me.

As I continued to pray and use prayer points that you send and some from Mountain of Fire site.

I made sure that I followed the guidelines you set about when and how to pray. I often start with quoting scriptures that were in your Prayer DNA.

Anyway, I knew in my spirit that God would make a way for me to buy my own house despite the fact that I had bad credit.

When He made a way for me to have a new car with zero payment down and a reasonable monthly payment. I knew there is nothing stopping my God from giving me a house.

So, I called my present Landlord to ask for an extension by one month (the Holy Spirit gave me this idea, and told me to tell her by faith that I'm moving into my own house and I needed more time). So I obeyed, she readily agreed and was very happy for me.

Meanwhile, nothing has happen yet. Two banks have turned me down and advise me to file for bankruptcy.

So, I asked the Lord if this is will, I'll obey. So I called my lawyer to setup appointment to file for bankruptcy.

Then I got an email from someone who I had written about a house he is selling. He told me he has someone who can help me get a loan to buy a house even with my bad credit. You know I've heard that before and everyone that said that always end up telling me my situation is too bad and would drop me like a ball.

Anyway, I called the number this man gave me, spoke to the loan officer. He said basically the same thing that other said except that he said, he knows some investors who would buy this house with their own credit and hand it over to me.

I would have to be making payment to them instead of the bank and my name would be on the house as an owner, which would evidently help improve my credit rating.

I leaped for joy. I agreed to it. He called me today and told me to start looking for a house that I want to live in because the investors are ready to move quickly.

Now, this is a BREAKTHROUGH.

GOD loves me, loves me, loves me!

Thank you, Elisha, for everything.

Sister Becky, Washington

"Five New Jobs Already . . . and We Only Started the Prayers 6 Weeks Ago!"

188

Elisha,

You sent the email on how to obtain your dream job, and I immediately printed it out and began applying the steps not only for myself, but for others as well.

In our area it's hard to find good paying jobs, as a lot of industries have shut down over the past few years. I got the email at the end of September, and since October 31, not just one or two of us have obtained jobs, but FIVE, and my interview is Friday morning!!!!

Two of these have since given up their jobs, but in that week, three jobs, the next week, two, and this week, my opportunity. The only hold up was testing and training we had to complete over a three week period, which means we actually got the invitations for this part IMMEDIATELY after putting the principles to work!!!

I don't know why, but one morning, your site just popped up when I started a search, and I can only say God put us together at the right time for a purpose.

Thank You, and God gets the glory, of course, but I will be ordering the prayer cookbook shortly.

Sister Laura, Texas

The simple biblical principles the Lord led me to share with these folks (and thousands of others) help do two things: they uncover the invisible "leaks" in your Spiritual Funnel, and show you how to instantly plug them through aggressive prayer. That means more blessings are delivered to you when you pray for them, and that means more of them manifest each time you pray.

They also help to expose the mistakes you are now making that—as with most struggling Christians—are interfering with the physical manifestation of their blessings. Just removing these spiritual roadblocks will increase the manifestation of God's promised blessings within a month.

Even more important, you learn how to increase the "magnetic power" of your prayers to the point that within a few weeks you can see double, triple, or even quadruple blessings than you used to get . . . and much, much more!

All this information has been packaged in a simple e-book that you can view online right now!

This is what one reader had to say:

"Totally Awesome . . . A Great Book"

> *Elisha,*
>
> *I just finished reading your book and I must say that it is awesome! I can already feel the changes that are going on within my body and my mind. Oh my goodness.*
>
> *All I can say is thank you, thank you, thank you. Totally Awesome!*
>
> *Jearnita, Atlanta*

Please take a look at this e-book while you are still thinking about it. Simply go to *www.prayerdnasecrets.com* and see for yourself.

OTHER BOOKS IN THE SERIES

BOOK FOUR

THE DREAM CODE

Knowing How to Cancel Bad Dreams When You
Wake Up Can Save Your Job, Your Home and
Even The Life of a Loved One . . . Someday.

$\mathcal{L}$et's begin with a true life story from Dubai:

> *"My name is John from Kenya. I work and live in Dubai and my wife lives in Kenya.*
>
> *On Saturday 24-01-09, I had a nightmare, I saw a very big fire burning down a business and I was about 50 metres away coming towards the burning business.*
>
> *Suddenly it turned out that my wife was in the burning business and I could see ambulances rescuing people from the burning shop.*
>
> *A person saw me and ran towards me stopping me from going near the fire and I noticed he was trying to stop me from seeing what was going on, since it seemed that one who looked like my wife was among the victims.*

Then an ambulance from the scene passed next to me heading to hospital and I noticed my wife in it, badly burned.

I woke up in great fear and I heard a soft voice telling me to cancel that nightmare.

I said, 'Let satanic fire be put off by the blood of Jesus, I evacuate my wife from satanic fire in Jesus name . . .' and I continued as the Holy Spirit enabled me.

On 27-01-09 I sent her some money which she was supposed to collect on 28-01-09 in Nairobi. On Friday 30-01-09, I called her to ask her whether she collected the money on 28th but she told me that she didn't go because there was a strong force stopping her from going.

Then she mentioned about a supermarket which exploded in flames in Nairobi on the day she was to collect the money.

About 30 people perished in the fire and the bank my wife collects the money from is some hundred metres from the supermarket.

She told me that everyday she goes to collect the money I send, she must go to the supermarket for some shopping and moreover the time it burned, coincided with the time she always go to collect the money.

All these she told me before I had told her of the nightmare I had.

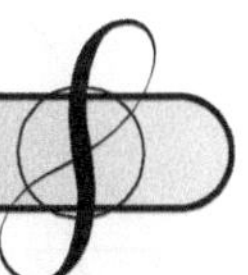

> *I thank our Lord Jesus for revealing this scheme of the devil and thank Him for you Elisha for before I knew your website, I didn't know anything about dreams, their meaning and how to cancel them.*
>
> *When she told me about the fire, I heard the same voice say 'remember the nightmare?'"*
>
> *John M., Dubai*

"I Had A Dream and Saw the Company Issuing Layoff Letters To Staff!"

> *"Somewhere in August 2008 our company due to hard economy conditions in the USA decided to give every worker a financial gift. At the same period I had a dream and saw our company issuing out letters and asking us to leave the company property!*
>
> *I did not understand it so I prayed for the meaning. I did not want to believe that the company which was dishing out monetary gift can at the same time send us away in lay-off or anything of that sort.*
>
> *In the course of my prayers my dream was confirmed when after September financial crisis in the country and my company started laying off workers!*

I kept on praying and survived two lay-offs last year. Everybody thought with two lay-offs it was over. But I kept on praying and fasting for 21 days from November to December 2008 and did Esther fast as well on two occasions with Psalms 27 and 91 you gave us.

On the 31ˢᵗ December after praying to close out the year in that special 27 minutes prayer program, I dreamed and saw myself among a group of people with a man dressed in white and everybody's hand was raised struggling to receive something from him.

Though I was standing at the back he still managed to find my hands from the raised hands and gave me the gift!

When everybody thought the lay-offs were over suddenly everybody in my company were giving WARNING LETTERS on Jan 9, 2009 for possible lay-off in March, 2009.

The affected individuals were to be informed on February 2, 2009 to proceed on leave for the lay-off in March 2009!

Then came the Feb 2, 2009 and about half of the work force were laid off but to God be the glory I was among the selected few people who were chosen to stay to work!

My manager then came to our office and shook my hands and congratulated me for being dedicated to work and that I am part of his plans so I am to remain and work! Praise God!"

Simon, Arizona

Some people still think that dreams mean nothing at all. Not true. You are about to discover that your dreams can help deliver timely information that you need and do it in a way that is all gain and no pain. You're about to see that dreams have been known to help many famous people achieve success and accomplish seemingly impossible feats. History shows that one of the most important ingredient of success is timely information.

The information I'm talking about here is the one you receive in your dreams. Here's how a few well-known people in history received the information that made them famous.

Christopher Columbus

Columbus dreamed he heard someone speak to him with the message, "God will give you the keys of the gates to the ocean, which are closed with strong chains!" The dream served as his launching pad and inspired him to plan a voyage westward. While searching for another route to the east, he ended up stumbling upon the New World—America.

Charles Dickens

 Legend has it that one night Charles Dickens, one of the world's greatest novelists, had a dream where he saw a woman in a red shawl with her back toward him. "I am Miss Napier," she said as she turned around to meet him with a broad smile.

197

Initially, the dream didn't mean anything to Dickens. But the next night, following a stage performance, some friends came backstage and introduced him to someone special they wanted him to meet. Her name was—you guessed it—Miss Napier. Dickens' dream helped him find love of his life.

Albert Einstein

Einstein's historian writes about this 20th century's greatest scientist whose dream literally changed the world:

> *"I was sledding with my friends at night. I started to slide down the hill but my sled started going faster and faster. I was going so fast that I realized I was approaching the speed of light. I looked up at that point and I saw the stars. They were being refracted into colors I had never seen before. I was filled with a sense of awe. I understood in some way that I was looking at the most important meaning in my life."*

Years later, Einstein recounted that his entire scientific career was built on the foundation of that dream.

What is the common thread in the lives of these famous individuals? They did not ignore their dreams. They had the will to act upon their dreams. They focused on their dreams like a laser and organized their lives to make their dreams a reality.

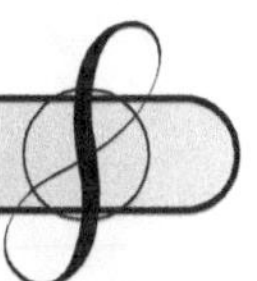

All dreams contain vital information and understanding them may be crucial to living a successful life. People who do not understand their dreams have the same desires as everyone else. But their lives may remain unfulfilled because they lack spiritual information that should help them succeed. Some dreams have even been known to help people solve scientific problems, paint a masterpiece, or improve at sports.

Your dreams can help you to:

- **Compose great songs**—One of the greatest composers who ever lived, Wolfgang Amadeus Mozart, said he received many of his astounding compositions through dreams.
- **Write great books**—The story is told of how Robert Louis Stevenson struggled for days over a short story that refused to make sense until a dream helped to give him clarity and that little story eventually transformed into the classic *Dr. Jekyll and Mr. Hyde.*
- **Invent cures for dreaded diseases**—If Dr. Jonas Salk had chosen to ignore his dreams, the polio vaccine might never have existed.
- **Improve at sport**—World champion golfer Jack Niklaus told a reporter in 1964 that a dream was instrumental to his championship success.

Whatever your desires are you need to have timely spiritual information and this information oftentimes is delivered in the dream.

But is this scriptural? You'll find at least 28 descriptions of dreams in the Bible. Famous Bible characters such as Joseph and Daniel were known for their ability to interpret dreams. There are many examples in the Bible in which God used dreams to convey vital information to people. *Very* famous characters, such as Solomon Joseph (in the Old and New Testaments)—and even in the life of our Lord Jesus.

Dreams Were Critical to the life and Death of Christ!

Today, God still uses dreams to pass important information to people. Now, how would you like to know, purely from a biblical perspective and in simple-to-understand language:

- ○ How to understand your dreams
- ○ How to recognize good and bad dreams
- ○ The nine dreams that bring riches, success and promotion
- ○ How to bring your good dreams into manifestation
- ○ How to cancel bad dreams
- ○ How to stop bad dreams

. . . and much, much more!

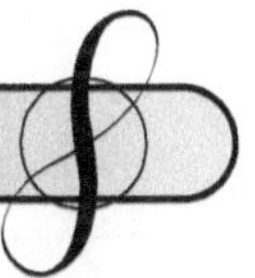

Today you can make the first step toward applying a long-lost biblical secret to understand your dreams. And best of all, you can take action to make your good dreams a reality while cancelling those that are bad and ugly. Just like the two examples described above.

Three Questions You Must Ask Yourself

Take a moment to ask yourself the following questions:

1. Am I ignoring my dreams?
2. Is it possible that God has already given me the key to my happiness in the dream and I did not recognize it?
3. Could I be the next Charles Dickens who found the love of his life or even the next Columbus who will receive the key to his own ocean of fame, success and happiness through the dream?

"Thank you for your teachings concerning dreams. After battling with a monster who was holding a young man captive in my dream. I was provoked to go to hospital to pray for HIV patients after a one week fasting and praying although I am not a pastor. In fact all the ten patients I prayed for tested negative, the doctors are now investigating their medical records."

Brother Innocent, Senegal

> *"Though I am a wide reader I have never come across books with such a deep revelation of the spiritual world. Your books are awesome, practical & not like any other I have read . . ."*
>
> *Lynette, South Africa*

For more details please visit: *www.the dreamcode.com*

Other Books in the Series

Book Five

The Number One Secret for Getting Out of Debt

$\mathcal{D}$o you find yourself up to your neck in debt, living from paycheck to paycheck? Here's how to move from debt into abundance, the scriptural way.

Let's begin with a typical email from an individual who diligently applied the principles in the book we are about to discuss:

> *"This is great news it is burning hot and I am glorifying and praising my God who is able to do exceedingly, abundantly above we can ask or think. Elisha I can hardly contain myself with this great news of what the Lord has done.*
>
> *I fasted and prayed for the Lord to relieve me of my financial debts. These debts were like a noose around my neck and I was not only living from paycheck to paycheck and at the end of the month I had to juggle to find out which bill I should pay with the little I had and which I should leave for the next paycheck.*

I counted up all my debts and totaled them and prayed and fasted with every fiber in my being and I told the Lord I know that He can deliver me and I trusted Him.

It is not yet ninety days and God has answered my prayer. My mountain of debt was ninety thousand dollars (90,000) and 'Glory to God' all my debts are paid and not only that I now have thirty thousand (30,000) dollars in the bank. Can you imagine that, Elisha? I had zero dollars in the bank. I have not had one thousand (1,000) dollars in the bank for a long, long, long time and imagine I now have thirty thousand (30,000) dollars.

God is truly amazing. Thank you Elisha, I wish I could talk to you and really explain this testimony in its entirety. From glory to glory He leads me on and I will continue to praise Him and thank Him and live my life totally for Him for there is victory and fullness in Jesus.

I am a single parent mom with twin daughters and we live in a very small house and I have been trying for years to be able to expand it so that we can have more room but because of these mountain of debts the banks have turned me down and I could not find the money or the know how to do it but I am convinced that Jesus will do it for me on my next project."

Sandra, Island of Belize

There is a way to pray yourself out of debt and into abundance, sometimes in as short a period as 90 days.

If you're reading this, then you probably realize you have the potential to get out of debt and begin to swim in the ocean of divine abundance. You may be looking for something that will help you become free from debt because God's promise for His children is that they will lend to nations and will not borrow.

I have a just-released product that will satisfy all your questions and get you on the road to being debt free *as fast as possible*. Here's a true statement:

The quality of life you experience as a Christian will be directly related to the quality of prayers you pray.

However, I'll let you in on a little secret into the formation of this very special prayer handbook. It includes material and prayers from our popular *Prayer Riot Series* which have helped many people around the world pray their way out of enormous debts and into financial abundance. Those who have participated in these 21-day intensive prayer sessions have reported that mountains of debt have been rolled off their back, sometimes within 90 days. And it includes a lot more.

The Number One Secret of Getting Out of Debt That Nobody Talks About will offer you more than just the spiritual tools to get you out of debt. It will connect you to the

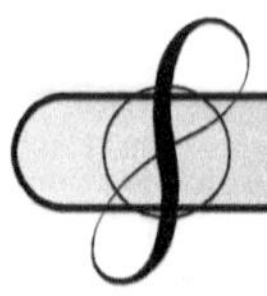

divine frequency of the Almighty and allow you to tap into God's storehouse for your everyday provisions, eliminating forever all scarcity and lack from your life.

Those who apply the 101 Precision Prayers (for getting out debt and into abundance) have received blessings such as you can see here:

> *"I gave some printouts to some friend who didn't bother to read it but gave it out to some cousin of hers, and this lady was deeply troubled with debts, unemployment but after reading it, she got a breakthrough. After three days, she got a job and cleared her debts. Glory be to God. Thanks a lot, it's not only working for me but even for people I don't know once they get down to it."*
>
> *Katushabe H., Uganda*
>
> *"God is good. The company I work for said they had no money to pay us a bonus. I have been praying for the Lord to release financial miracles into my life. Well on Friday I received twenty thousand Dollars ($20,000). To God be the glory."*
>
> *Carlene H., Kingston, Jamaica*

> *"This is right in line with what my pastor has been teaching on effectual, power prayers that get results . . . we have numerous testimonies, the largest thus far being a $23,000 debt cancellation!!"*
>
> *Sharon F., United States*

The Most Effective Prayer Secret, Ever!

Can I ask you something? Would you like to have the divine ability to:

- Harvest so much unexpected finances that you will be able to pay off *all* your debts and still live comfortably on the rest, just like in the Bible?
- Wake up every morning, excited about your day, knowing the Lord has truly appointed people you don't even know to bless you?
- Have complete strangers approach you and give you precisely the information that you need to generate new wealth? (Remember how, in the Bible, an angel of God revealed the secret of wealth creation to Jacob in the dream!)
- Receive turnaround breakthroughs in your career, business, and in your relationships?
- Know how to slam the door shut against financial embarrassment?

209

○ Be the trusted adviser people can turn to for help
when they need spiritual direction?

Then you need to read my just-released handbook: *The
#1 Secret of Getting Out of Debt That Nobody Talks About: 101
Precision Prayers to Move You Out of Debt Into Abundance.* In
this prayer manual you will find the scriptural key to the
door that opens a closet with an endless supply of divine
blessings, miracles and testimonies. Readers have said that
this is one of the most amazing spiritual blueprint on this
topic to ever exist. It changes the way you see prayer and
empowers you to take advantage of this God-given but long-
neglected gift.

In this 86-page handbook you will find a breakdown,
chapter-by-chapter, of this prayer principle that has helped
hundreds of Christians just like you to finally disentangle
themselves from the evil web of debt and realize their
dreams of divine supply and abundance.

Inside the handbook you'll find how seven simple steps
that can help you see the power of the Precision Prayer.

> *"Remember the block of land I told you we've been trying to sell
> for months without success? After my Esther Fast on Monday, the
> bank rang my husband on Tuesday with an offer from this one
> buyer . . . and we just made a tidy profit of $50,459.75!"*
>
> *Sister Sisi, Australia*

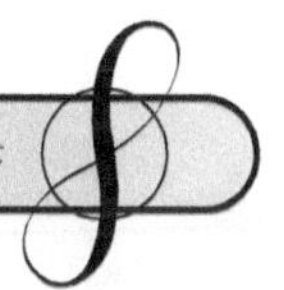

What Is "Precision Praying" Anyway?

Precision (or targeted) praying is a practical, Bible-based method that allows *any* persistent Christian from any denominational background to receive answers to their prayers—sometimes in as short a period as 21 days.

> *"My husband and I were involved in the 21-day prayer marathon. Within 3 weeks, we had our first major breakthrough! We had a very unexpected resource send a check in the amount of $5,000! This is the exact amount I had prayed for. We give God the glory!! Thank you so very much for teaching others the 'scriptural way' of prayer. God bless you continually."*
>
> Cindy H., Ohio

This handbook is a spiritual roadmap to show you and help you make the transition from debt to abundance AS FAST AS POSSIBLE, but you must be willing to pray the prayers. For more details please visit *www.prayoutofdebt.com*.

211

"I spotted the Word of God in Deuteronomy 15 for cancelling debts. I wrote down the list of people who owed me money and I forgave them. Then I took days off duty and went on Esther's fast option as well.

The following week was full of miracles. People I owed money called me and forgave me big percentages. This was overwhelmingly great and it reduced the amount I owed them. I had debts of about 20,000,000 million shillings (almost $9,000) which accrued from borrowing from money lenders.

I had to repent for having borrowed because we are supposed to be lenders not borrowers. This epidemic made me a non-payer of my tithe and was draining my savings, my joy and plans. This was the weapon the devil was using to distract my ministry of evangelism through book writing. I became a humble borrower living on advanced paychecks.

The cancer of debts goes with time because they came in slowly also. I am now stabilizing with time and have had the opportunity to write down my experiences during this time (5) and eventually got inspirations and make them into testimonial booklets of how the Holy Spirit would lead me to win situations.

The Holy Spirit is such a good companion that I have become totally dependent on seeking advice on every step of event I take. I will post you a few samples of my 1ˢᵗ book. I yet have 5 more series to publish and I am still writing more. People are requesting for French and Swahili versions and even local languages."

Rosemary K., Uganda

OTHER BOOKS IN THE SERIES

BOOK SIX

Prayer of Caleb

> *"I wanted to let you know, from our conversation a couple of months ago, you shared with me that if I prayed the prayer of peace for Jerusalem, I would experience a financial breakthrough within 60 days. Do you remember that conversation? I was discouraged about my finances and you shared with me there were ways other than tithing and 'seed money' to experience financial breakthroughs?*
>
> *Within 60 days, true to what the Holy Spirit led you to share with me, I did receive several financial breakthroughs. Hallelujah!! I prayed for 60 days a specific prayer for Jerusalem during the "midnight hour" and God surely turned things around."*
>
> *Marina W., Chicago*

When Christians online need urgent turnaround breakthroughs the Holy Spirit leads them to *www.firesprings.com*.

When they feel discouraged, like God is far away from them, and all roads seem to lead nowhere, no matter what they try, the Holy Spirit leads them to this site.

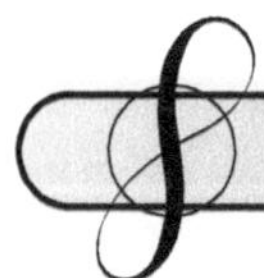

When poor health or chronic sickness is slowly squeezing life out of them (or someone they know) and the doctors have practically given up on them, the Holy Spirit leads them to this website.

Only a few short weeks later (or even days), most of them have something to say, such as in the following praise report:

> *"A quick note to let you know that I started my new job on Monday 9th October 2006, after 44 days of prayer and fasting which included the 21 days of Prayer Marathon (and of course the 3-day Esther fast). I am very grateful to God for this because this is the first time in 14 years since I obtained my PhD degree that I have a permanent job with an automatic monthly salary."*
>
> *Beatrice, London, UK*

Can you now guess why the Holy Spirit leads all these folks to our website? Prayer Bullets.

Meaning: Prayer Points that Work . . . PLUS HOW and WHEN to pray them!

Why is this crucially important for you? Because it's a known fact; a cardinal truth in the realm of the spirit, that *there is NO spiritual problem that cannot be solved with the right prayer point.*

If you are reading this letter now, you did not get it by accident. The Holy Spirit put this manual into your hands to show you the way *out* of your problems; to help wipe away those secret tears that you cry when no one else is around. Literally, when you agree to follow this prayer "prescription" . . . you receive prayer points that target and directly address your most challenging problems, plus HOW and WHEN to use them for the answers to manifest in the shortest possible time.

The Results? An intimate spiritual walk with the LORD, finances released, poverty uprooted, spanking new homes, godly spouses, brand new cars, dramatic healings, new jobs, debts cancelled, and much, much more.

Since I went online to share these little-known secrets of prayer, I have received over 1,975 documented testimonies like the ones here, plus countless others on the phone (as at the time of writing). What's more, when we were doing the *Prayer Marathon* sessions a few years back, it became clear to me that some form of hands-on mentoring and coaching was needed to get some folks over the top.

And, praise the Lord, as soon as I added that one missing element, our websites recorded more testimonies within a three-week period than at any other time since we went online.

Why? Because even the most diligent, prayerful believer can hit a brick wall and become discouraged, praying, praying, and believing God for a breakthrough. Sometimes, you're just too close to the problem to realize that the answer to your prayers has already arrived—in coded form, through dreams or visions.

Other times, you simply need the help and agreement of others to quicken, or push, your breakthrough into open manifestation, such as this next example:

> *"Do you remember me telling you about the vision of people giving me money and then this particular lady gave $1,000.00 but the big black bird came to snatch it away from my hand! But I went ahead and command the 'Angelic Executioner of God to execute the bird and also command the fire of God to burn it to ashes.'*
>
> *Well just after finishing that prayer on the 9th . . . the next day I received $1,572.00 in check. And on Thursday . . . after work I went to the bank to withdraw some of my wages to buy our weekly groceries . . . guess how much was in my bank account!!! $8,000.00. At first I thought someone has put that money in the wrong account but we found out later it is definitely mine."*
>
> *Sisilia H., Australia*

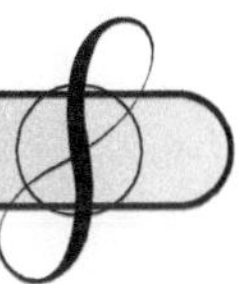

Recently we held a special Prayer Marathon targeted at restoring health and youthfulness. The Lord made it such a success that I created a book out of it.

Here are three good reasons why you need to at least have a look at this book:

Good Reason #1—Just glancing through this easy-to-read material lays bare the three ancient secrets of anti-aging that Bible characters utilized to stay perpetually young, strong, and healthy; from Sarah, to Anna, to Moses, to Caleb.

This biblical, *proven* "roadmap" for staying young, healthy, and disease-free is critical now more than ever. Expensive, complex wellness solutions that are beyond your budget won't do you any good. What most of us need is useable "divine health principles and prayer advice" that can be put into action right now. Without needing to hunt for expensive consultations, or be forced to buy high-priced medication/cosmetics, or spend your money on things you don't really need.

Good Reason #2—If you are currently facing any health-related problem (or you know anyone who is) it is important for you to realize that today's healthcare programs are *not* set up to cure you of most ailments completely. Only Jesus has an abiding interest in your total wellness and wholeness.

Those who manufacture some of the medication you take could be more interested in helping you manage your problems, instead of simply giving you an all-out, one-time cure. That way they hope to keep you a loyal customer until you go to the grave, while they grow fatter and richer at your expense. Talk about modern day slavery—only today it's the big pharmaceutical companies and their agents.

In this slim, result-focused book (it's only 108 pages but it packs real power), I explain step-by-step how you can apply scriptural secrets of divine health to effect gradual and total restoration of your health, while renewing your youth; like that of an eagle's.

> *"I thank God for what you are doing in my life. I have learned to create a personal relationship with God from your prayers and instructions. I have suffered a lot for my one year as a Christian, running after men of God who are never available to pray for me. Man of God you have really mentored me to grow in my spiritual life to another level which is frightening my relatives and friends!"*
>
> *Salamatu S., Cameroon*

> *"First of all I would like to say 'Thank You.' It has been a powerful week. On today, my son tried to commit suicide at school. Earlier this morning the Holy Spirit had spoken to me and told me to begin to pray for my son because the devil planned to kill him. I don't remember what I prayed but it was a prayer point . . ."*
>
> *Lodie Q., N. Carolina*

For more details, please visit: *www.firesprings.com.*